COURT OFFICER

NEW YORK STATE

(NYS COURT OFFICER-TRAINEE)

by

Success Education Team

Focused and clear

exam preparation guides

"Court Officer New York State"

and

"NYS Court Officer-Trainee"

•

Court Officers in New York State are NYS civil service employees
and work in courts throughout New York State.

To be canvassed for pre-hiring screening, a candidate must take the
"New York State Court Officer-Trainee Exam"
and score high enough to be considered for appointment.
(For simplicity, we will refer to both Court Officers and
Court Officer-Trainees as "Court Officers.")

If candidates pass the required physical, medical and background investigations, and other
requirements, they may choose the area of NYS where they wish to be assigned.

ISBN: 9781091155510

The web addresses and information in this book are current as of the date of publishing. The web addresses and
information may change as time goes on. Please refer to the current official web sites and official publications for
current information. The examples and questions in this book are for exam study purposes and do not contain any
official policies, names, rules, codes, or procedures of any public agency or department, or any private business
or governmental entity. All names, locations and addresses are fictional and any similarity between names in this
book and real persons or places is coincidental.

(1) "Sample Examination Questions" (NYS Office of Court Administration 2014)
(2) Court Officer-Trainee Exam Announcement (2014)
(3) http://www.courts.state.ny.us/careers/cot/ and www.nycourts.gov/courtofficer-recruit
(4) Wikipedia.org
(5) firesafe.org.uk
Cover image: Fotolia.com

CONTENTS

CHAPTER 1: Introduction

Why this book is better!

1. **This book is SPECIFICALLY for the 2020 New York State Court Officer-Trainee Exam.**

2. It is the result of extensive collaboration among current and retired New York State Court Officers and New York State Court employees with many years of service.

3. It excludes unnecessary and time-wasting information about exams in other states.

4. It covers all the types of questions listed on the NYS prior exam announcement.

5. It covers the post-exam medical, physical, and investigation hiring process.

6. Each section starts with a practice exercise for you to assess your knowledge and performance on each type of question.

7. Practice questions are explained and analyzed - and valuable hints are provided.

8. A full practice exam with the answers explained is also included.

ALL YOU NEED TO BE SUCCESSFUL!

"The will to win, the desire to succeed, the urge to reach your full potential – these are the keys that will unlock the door...."

- Confucius

What is a good score on the exam??????

The following canvassing information is from the nycourts.gov website: (Visit the website for the most current information.)

"CANVASSING INFORMATION FOR 2014 EXAM #45-784
(As of April 16, 2019)

LOCATION PREFERENCES/AVAILABILITY INQUIRY CANVASS:
On April 16, 2019, eligible candidates who scored a 70 or above on the 2014 written examination for List #45-784 were canvassed via email. Candidates were asked to submit a location preference form and select one of four work regions to be considered for appointment:

I. Judicial Districts 3 - 8
II. 9th Judicial District
III. 10th Judicial District
IV. New York City (All Boroughs)
If you received a score of 70 or above and have not received an email, please email ASM@NYCOURTS.GOV

THE FOLLOWING CANDIDATES HAVE BEEN OFFERED CONDITIONAL APPOINTMENTS AND ARE BEGINNING THE SCREENING PROCESS:
NYC ALL BOROUGHS:
Rank #'s 3 - 9179 (Score 88 and above)

JUDICIAL DISTRICTS 3 - 8:
Rank #'s 1 - 26247 (Score 80.5 and above)*

*ONLY CANDIDATES WITH A SCORE OF 91 AND ABOVE WERE REACHED FOR THE LATEST CANVASS.

9th JUDICIAL DISTRICT:
Rank #'s 12-11799 (Score of 88 and above)

10TH JUDICIAL DISTRICT:
Rank #'s 2-9180 (Score 88 or above)"

---

1. From the above, one might conclude that to be canvassed in New York City or its vicinity, a higher score is needed than for upstate counties.

2. In New York City, candidates should aim for a score of 88 or above. Lower than that, they may have to wait a much longer time to be canvassed, or may not be canvassed at all.

To maximize your score, study this book carefully - and, if you have time, practice with the extra questions and answers in our companion book, "COURT OFFICER NEW YORK STATE (NYS COURT OFFICER-TRAINEE) WORKBOOK."

The Court Officer Job

Court Officers
- are New York State employees
- are trained uniformed peace officers
- are certified and authorized to carry firearms

Court officers are assigned to courts throughout New York State. Most are assigned to courts within New York City. However, a constantly growing number are assigned to courts throughout the state (Nassau and Suffolk Counties, and Judicial Districts 3, 4, 5, 6, 8, and 9). Court Officers are not currently assigned to the 7th Judicial District.

To be **appointed** as a Court Officer-Trainee, you must be:
> At least 20.5 years of age (This age was increased from the age in the 2014 announcement.)
> A United States citizen and a resident of New York State

You must possess a High School diploma or equivalent and a valid New York State Driver's License.

(Note: The 2014 Court Officer-Trainee Exam Number: 45-784 does not state any minimum age or education requirement to **take** the test. However, there are minimum education and age requirements to start working as a Court Officer. These requirements may change. Please see the current exam announcement for any changes.)

Although the main duties of Court Officers relate to court security in offices, courtrooms and public areas, Court Officers also perform other duties, including some clerical duties in courtrooms.

Court Officers are usually the first court employees that court visitors see. Because of this, the professional and impartial way that Court Officers carry out their duties is important in maintaining the public's positive attitude and confidence in the court system.

In public areas, they may work at magnetometer screening posts, where they aid the flow of court visitors and often respond to inquiries from the public and attorneys. Because of this, Court Officers must be familiar with court procedures and must be able to apply interpersonal skills.

Generally, one or two Court Officers are assigned to every Civil Court and Family Court courtroom. These Court Officers often respond to inquiries from the public and may at times make oral announcements. They may also call court calendars and assist in transporting court files.

In some criminal courtrooms, four or five or more Court Officers may be assigned. In these courtrooms, a Court Officer Sergeant usually supervises the officers. In all courtrooms, Court Officers may at times assist other court employees in carrying out their duties.

In jury trial parts, Court Officers help to maintain jury integrity. They must be vigilant in maintaining a fair and impartial demeanor. Many times, and especially during jury deliberations, they act as the intermediaries between the jurors and the judge.

Exam Announcement*

The Court Officer-Trainee exam is usually announced by the New York State Office of Court Administration at least four or five months (or more) before the exam date. The exam announcement usually contains information about the following:
- Starting Salary
- Application
- Examination Administration Dates
- Distinguishing Features of Work
- Minimum Qualifications for Appointment
- Eligible List and Location of Positions
- Benefits
- Physical, Medical and Other Requirements

There is usually a page of additional information on: Application, Filing Fee, Veteran Credits, Verification of Qualifications, Examination Ratings, Special Arrangements, and a Warning regarding unethical or illegal exam practices. (See current exam announcement.)

The following edited details are from the Court Officer-Trainee Exam Announcement (2014) and the NYS Courts website. (Please review the current announcement for the most up-to-date information.)

Starting Salary
Starting Court Officer Trainee salary (April 2019) is : $50,112 + approximately up to $4,000 (location pay in NYC - Metropolitan Area).

Application
There is a fee for applying for the exam. The amount is stated on the exam announcement. Fee may be waived under certain circumstances. Both the application and application fee must be filed electronically on the web site stated on the exam announcement.
A credit card (or debit card) and applicant's email address are usually required.

IMPORTANT

"An application is considered filed upon immediate receipt of an Application ID Number."(2)
(You should receive the application ID Number immediately by confirmation email after you file the application. This is your proof that you filed the application. Keep it in a safe place in case you need it.)

Examination Administration Dates
Usually, one or two exam dates are provided. The dates (and location of exam site) are usually randomly assigned and are emailed to all candidates by a specified date.

(From the last page of the exam announcement)(2)

"CANDIDATES SHOULD CONTACT THE CIVIL SERVICE ADMINISTRATION OFFICE AT CIVILSERVICEADMIN@NYCOURTS.GOV IF THE ADMISSION NOTICE HAS NOT BEEN RECEIVED BY (SPECIFIED DATE)."

* 2014 exam announcement

Distinguishing Features of Work

"New York State Court Officer-Trainees serve a two-year traineeship during which time they are responsible for maintaining order and providing security in courtrooms, court buildings and grounds. They work under the direct supervision of a NYS Court Officer-Sergeant and the general supervision of the court clerk or other security supervisory personnel. After completion of formal training at the Academy, NYS Court Officer-Trainees may be assigned to all trial courts and court agencies to begin the on-the-job training portion of their two-year traineeship. NYS Court Officer-Trainees are peace officers, required to wear uniforms, and may be authorized to carry firearms, execute bench warrants and make arrests. Typical duties include: guarding and escorting criminal defendants while in the court facility; escorting judges, juries and witnesses; handling court documents and forms; providing information and assistance to the public and other court users; maintaining the security of deliberating and sequestered juries; displaying and safeguarding exhibits; operating security equipment and using established search procedures; physically restraining and calming unruly individuals; administering first-aid and assistance to individuals during emergencies; and performing related duties."[2]

Minimum Qualifications for Appointment

A candidate **AT THE TIME OF APPOINTMENT** must meet all of the following qualifications:
- Have a high school diploma or the equivalent
- Be at least 20.5 years old
- Be a citizen of the United States
- Have a valid New York State Driver's License

Eligible List and Location of Positions

Candidates who pass the exam are included in an eligible list. The candidates are listed in descending order according to the score on the test (plus any veterans credits). They are appointed to positions in courts statewide.
(Note: Candidates are usually asked to indicate their preference as to the NYS geographical area where they wish to be assigned.)

Benefits include the following:
- New York State retirement system
- New York State Health Insurance Plan
- 20 paid holidays for the first year (and usually increasing one additional day per year for the next seven years).
- 12 paid holidays and liberal sick days
- *and other benefits (for example: dental benefits are provided by some unions).*

Physical and Medical Requirements

"Physical, medical, and psychological examinations will be conducted to ensure that candidates are able to satisfactorily perform the duties of this position. The examinations will include a fitness test, medical and psychological evaluations and substance abuse screening. For further information about the current physical standards and screening process, visit [3]
http://www.courts.state.ny.us/careers/cot/ or **www.nycourts.gov/courtofficer-recruit**

(The date that applications "<u>must be filed by</u>" is also stated on the exam announcement.)

The Exam

● 1. This three to four-hour exam is not an easy exam. However, if you studied with this book, you will have a tremendous advantage over those candidates who did not study properly. Therefore, the day before the exam, try to relax and get a good night's sleep. This is easily said, but sometimes not easily done as the exam is usually given on Saturdays and the traditional party night is Friday night.

● 2. Because this exam does not require prior memorization of facts and figures, there is no need to "cram". If you remember and apply the techniques in this book for answering the different types of questions, you will probably be successful.

● 3. Try to keep in mind that mass transit schedules and traffic flow are usually different on Saturdays and Sundays. Give yourself plenty to time to arrive at the test site **early**. If you can, travel to the test site at least a few days before the exam to see if any transportation problems might arise the day of the exam.

● 4. Especially if you are very experienced taking civil service exams and have done this "many times before," be careful and do NOT assume anything or take anything for granted. Read signs posted on the walls or doors and pay attention to all directions, oral or written.

● 5. Prior Court Officer-Trainee exams have been in written form (not computer). You are given a test booklet and an answer sheet that will later be scored by a computer scanner. When you are allowed to do so, check the answer sheet and the booklet to make sure there are no defects like missing pages in the booklet and dirty areas on the answer sheet that might interfere with the computer scanning the sheet. If there is a problem, bring it to the attention of the test monitor.

● 6. Make sure you know which questions you need to answer. (For example: 1-100, 1-95, etc.) Check the answer sheet to see in what direction the question numbers are listed, for example:

ANSWER SHEET				
1.	2.	3.	4.	5.
6.	7.	8.	9.	10. etc.

ANSWER SHEET		
1.	6.	11.
2.	7.	12.
3.	8.	13.
4.	9.	14.
5.	10.	15. etc.

• 7. Take a simple watch to the test. (Smart watches are usually not allowed.) Simple, either digital or the old fashioned analog watches, are fine. You need a watch to pace yourself during the test. Do not rely on the proctor to announce the time or to post the time on the blackboard in any helpful manner. Chances are, they won't. In establishing a time budget to answer the questions, remember that some questions, such as the record keeping ("table information") questions, take much longer than other questions.

• 8. Make sure that you mark each answer correctly (not too light, not too dark). Try to keep your answer sheet clean, without smudges. If you change an answer, make sure you erase the wrong answer completely. Computers do not have a conscience and can easily mistake a smudge for an answer. Also, remember to darken only one space for each question. Even if you think that there are two correct answers, just choose the one that you consider to be the best.

• 9. Periodically check that you are not skipping questions or answering in the wrong area of the answer sheet. If you feel you are getting too nervous, take a minute break and take deep breaths. Use the restroom as soon as you feel the need to do so. Feel tired? Take a bite out of a chocolate or any candy that you can eat quickly so that the act of chewing does not distract you.

• 10. If you studied correctly and budgeted your time efficiently on the test, you will probably finish with time to spare. However, do not just get up and go home. Stay until all the time has expired. Check, check, and triple-check your answers. One point can make a big difference on your rank on the list of successful candidates.

Exam Results

All answer forms will be graded and a list of successful candidates will be published by the Office of Court Administration. The time to grade the exam and publish the list will depend greatly on the availability of human resources at the Office of Court Administration Examinations Unit. (The latest list came out in 2015.) If you are confident that you did well on the exam, you may want to review the post-exam procedures that all candidates must go through. You should read all the requirements and see which areas you may need to address or improve before you receive a letter informing you that you are in the next group for pre-hiring screening.

How high do you have to score to be called for the pre-hiring screening process?

(See Page 5 for hiring details.)

(Study with this book to increase your chances of getting a 90+ score!)

__Post-Exam Procedures (In order)__

Generally, Court Officer-Trainee candidates must successfully complete the following steps.
(These requirements are historical and may change, therefore review the most recent requirements.)
These steps (the order of which is flexible) are listed on the official NYCOURTS.GOV website:
__http://ww2.nycourts.gov/careers/cot/screening4.shtml__
and other NYS Office of Court Administration resources.

Phase 1:
Physical Ability Test
Vision Test
Fingerprints

Phase 2:
Written Psychological Tests
Background Investigation

Phase 3:
Psychological Interview
Evaluation Board

Phase 4:
Pre-Appointment Medical Exam
Appointment to Academy

__NOTICE: The following are brief descriptions of some post-exam screening procedures.__
__For complete official and up-to-date information, please consult with the NYS Office of Court__
__Administration, including their correspondence unit, publications and websites.__

__"Phase 1__

Physical Ability Test includes push-ups. Illinois Agility Run, Sit-ups and Beep Test
Vision Test Near vision and far vision must be within prescribed limits.
Fingerprints will be taken and a $75 fee will be charged to all candidates.

__Phase 2__

Written Psychological Tests and a psychological interview are required.
Background Investigation (Conducted by the Applicant Verification & Compliance Unit)

__Phase 3__

Psychological Interview (conducted by a licensed clinical psychologist)
Evaluation Board (A review will be done by a panel of court mangers, security professionals, and
administrative staff.)

__Phase 4__

Pre-Appointment Medical Exam Comprehensive medical examination with a licensed physician.
Appointment to Academy (Candidates must be at least 20.5 years of age and possess a valid NYS
Driver's license.)"

NYS Court Officers Academy

The Court Officers Academy trains the approximately 4,500 NYS Court Officers and other court system non-uniformed peace officers.

Initial peace officer training (14 weeks) may be at the Court Officers Academy. There, Court Officer-Trainees undergo a program of physical, firearms, and academic training, including instruction in the NYS Penal Law, Criminal Law, and department policies and guidelines. During their career, Court Officers also receive on-going statewide training programs.

•

SALARY

(As of April 2020)

Court Officer-Trainee

Starting hiring rate : $ 51,113 plus up to approx. $ 4,000 location pay (New York City - Metropolitan Area).

Court Officer

After 2 years, Court Officer-Trainees are promoted to Line 19, "Court Officer".

Maximum pay for Court Officer (2nd Longevity) is $ 87,681 (after all yearly increases) plus up to approximately $ 4,000 location pay (New York City - Metropolitan Area).

Many Court Officers promote to higher-paying "Court Clerk" titles (Senior Court Clerk, Associate Court Clerk, and Principal Court Clerk).

Highest pay for "Principal Court Clerk" is $ 124,096 plus up to approximately $ 4,000 location pay (New York City - Metropolitan Area).

(The salary schedule usually increases every year.)

CHAPTER 2 : Types of questions on exam

On prior exams, 5 types of questions have usually been asked:

1. **Clerical Checking**
2. **Reading and Understanding Written Material**
   Format A: Understanding the content of a written passage
   Format B: Select the best alternative from four alternatives
   that best completes a sentence or passage.
3. **Applying Facts and Information to Given Situations**
4. **Remembering Facts and Information**
5. **Record Keeping**

How many questions of each type might there be on the exam?
The following is our best **GUESS** estimate:

Question Type	Approximate Number of Questions
1. Clerical Checking	15 - 20
2. Reading and Understanding Written Material: Format A: Understanding the content of a written passage	10
Reading and Understanding Written Material: Format B: Select the best alternative from four alternatives that best completes a sentence or passage.	10
3. Applying Facts and Information to Given Situations	10 - 20
4. Remembering Facts and Information	10 - 15
5. Record Keeping	15
Approximate Total Questions	**70 - 90**

Description of Types of Questions

Question Type	Description
1. Clerical Checking	"This section of the examination assesses your ability to determine whether different sets of words, numbers, names and codes are similar. No matter what the form of the item, you are required to scan the sets of information, identify where the sets differ, and use the directions to determine the correct answer."[1]
2. Reading and Understanding Written Material **Format A** **Understanding the content of a written passage**	"In this format, each question contains a brief reading selection followed by a question or questions pertaining to the information in the selection. All of the information required to answer the question(s) is provided, so even if the reading selection is on a topic with which you are not familiar, you will be able to answer the question(s) by reading the selection carefully."[1]
Format B **Select the best alternative from four alternatives that best completes a sentence or passage.**	"In this format the test contains a short, written passage from which some words have been omitted. You need to select one word from the four alternatives that best completes the passage."[1]
3. Applying Facts and Information to Given Situations	"This section of the written exam assesses your ability to take information which you have read and apply it to a specific situation defined by a given set of facts. Each question contains a brief passage which describes a regulation, procedure or law. The selection is followed by a description of a specific situation. Then a question is asked which requires you to apply the law, regulation, or procedure described in the passage to the specific situation."[1]

Question Type	Description
4. Remembering Facts and Information	"You will be provided with a written description of an incident (story) and given five (5) minutes to read and study the story. At the end of the 5-minute period, the story will be removed and you will not have another opportunity to refer back to it. You will not be permitted to make any written notes about the story. There will be a 10-minute delay before you receive your test question booklet. You will then be asked a series of questions about the facts concerning the story."(1)
5. Record Keeping	"These questions will assess your ability to read, combine and manipulate written information organized from several different sources."(1) The information is usually presented in a series of tables. **(Many candidates consider this to be the most difficult part of the test**.)

!

HINT

Some parts of the exam are more difficult than others and may require that you spend more time on each question.
This is especially true for the "Record Keeping" questions.
Practice these questions carefully and try to determine how much time to allow for them.

CHAPTER 3: CLERICAL CHECKING

The Office of Court Administration describes the clerical checking questions as follows:

"This section of the examination assesses your ability to determine whether different sets of words, numbers, names and codes are similar. No matter what the form of the item, you are required to scan the sets of information, identify where the sets differ, and use the directions to determine the correct answer."[1]

The instructions on the test for these questions are similar to the following:

Instructions

Questions 1-5 (below) consist of three sets of information. Compare the information in each set and mark your answer sheet, as follows:

Mark: Choice A if all three sets are different
Choice B if only the first and second sets are different
Choice C if only the first and third sets are different
Choice D if all the three sets are exactly alike.

Although this seems simple, it is not. Many test-takers lose valuable points on this section.

The reason for this will be clear to you after you complete the first 10 practice questions.

HINT

The better a reader you are, the more likely it is that you might make more mistakes in answering these types of questions. The reason is that good readers are usually *FAST* readers - and more likely to gloss over differences. Therefore, take the necessary (reasonable) time to make 100% sure of your answer.

Example 1 Instructions: Questions 1-5 (below) consist of three sets of information. Compare the information in each set and mark your answer sheet, as follows:

Mark: Choice A if all three sets are exactly alike
        Choice B if only the first and second sets are exactly alike
        Choice C if only the first and third sets are exactly alike
        Choice D if none of the three sets are exactly alike.

To simulate test conditions, answer questions 6-10 without first looking at the answers for questions 1-5.

1. Hazton, Spitzdorf, & Hines
   Surrogates Court Pub. 18K
   2852 Mahasset, Suite 3A-4
   New York, NY 10029-2568
   ID #: 486759-2019 (D)

2. 797554-437958 KCV-25
   Chambers 8635, 9829, 1035
   CPLR 1002 and CPL 3472 (g)
   2/29/18, 4/12/20, 3/7/21
   3749 Elmington Drive, (PA)

3. Lt. James Reichelder, Sr.
   Court Clerk E. Gradefelder
   Witness: Gregory F. Boulder
   Evidence Rep. 3917: 2 Folio
   F: 2857930-892 (Series A-B)

4. Services Report K-9721979
   Court Clerk H. Womenski
   JHO James Williamson
   Seq. (TA-1 - 4893234)
   Wasserman and Brystol

5. Brooklyn, NY 11246-2019
   JHO F. Schneider-Hamilton
   783-07-2203 and 978-4
   Rooms (307), (448)
   Surrogates Procedures 2020

---

1. Hazton, Spitzdorf, & Hines
   Surrogates Court Pub. 18K
   2852 Mahasset, Suite 3A-4
   New York, NY 10029-2568
   ID #: 486729-2019 (D)

2. 797554-437958 KCV-25
   Chambers 8635, 9829, 1035
   CPLR 1002 and CPL 3472 (g)
   2/29/18, 4/12/20, 3/7/21
   3749 Elmington Drive, (PA)

3. *Lt. James Reichelder, Sr.*
   Court Clerk E. Gradefelder
   Witness: Gregory F. Boulder
   Evidence Rep. 3917: 2 Folio
   F: 2857930-892 (Series A-B)

4. Services Report K-9721979
   Court Clerk H. Womanski
   JHO James Williamson
   Seq. (TA-1 - 4893234)
   Wasserman and Brystol

5. Brooklyn, NY 11246-2019
   JHO F. Schneider-Hamilton
   783-07-2203 and 978-4
   Rooms (307), (448)
   Surrogates Procedures 2020

---

1. Hazton, Spitzdorf, & Hines
   Surrogates Court Pub. 18K
   2852 Mahasset, Suite 3A-4
   New York, NY 10029-2568
   ID #: 486759-2019 (D)

2. 797554-437958 KCV-25
   Chambers 8635, 9829, 1035
   CPLR 1002 and CPL 3472 (g)
   2/29/18, 4/12/20, 3/7/21
   3749 Elmimgton Drive, (PA)

3. Lt. James Reichelder, Sr.
   Court Clerk E. Gradefelder
   Witness: Gregory F. Boulder
   Evidence Rep. 3917: 2 Folio
   F: 2857930-892 (Series A-B)

4. Services Report K-9721979
   Court Clerk H. Womensky
   JHO James Williamson
   Seq. (TA-1 - 4893234)
   Wasserman and Brystol

5. Brooklyn, NY 11246-2019
   JHO F. Schneider-Hamilton
   738-07-2203 and 978-4
   Rooms (307), (448)
   Surrogates Procedures 2020

Answer Sheet

1.A O B O C O D O
2.A O B O C O D O
3.A O B O C O D O
4.A O B O C O D O
5.A O B O C O D O

Answers are on next page.

There is something in the above 5 questions that makes many candidates confused and makes them answer incorrectly.

Can you tell what that is? (See the answer to question 3 on the next page.)

!

Court Officer New York State (NYS Court Officer Trainee)

Answers 1 - 5

1. Hazton, Spitzdorf, & Hines
   Surrogates Court Pub. 18K
   2852 Mahasset, Suite 3A-4
   New York, NY 10029-2568
   ID #: 486759-2019 (D)

2. 797554-437958 KCV-25
   Chambers 8635, 9829, 1035
   CPLR 1002 and CPL 3472 g)
   2/29/18, 4/12/20, 3/7/21
   3749 Elmington Drive, (PA)

3. Lt. James Reichelder, Sr.
   Court Clerk E. Gradefelder
   Witness: Gregory F. Boulder
   Evidence Rep. 3917: 2 Folio
   F: 2857930-892 (Series A-B)

4. Services Report K-9721979
   Court Clerk H. **Womenski**
   JHO James Williamson
   Seq. (TA-1 - 4893234)
   Wasserman and Brystol

5. Brooklyn, NY 11246-2019
   JHO F. Schneider-Hamilton
   783-07-2203 and 978-4
   Rooms (307), (448)
   Surrogates Procedures 2020

---

1. Hazton, Spitzdorf, & Hines
   Surrogates Court Pub. 18K
   2852 Mahasset, Suite 3A-4
   New York, NY 10029-2568
   ID #: 486**729**-2019 (D)

2. 797554-437958 KCV-25
   Chambers 8635, 9829, 1035
   CPLR 1002 and CPL 3472 g)
   2/29/18, 4/12/20, 3/7/21
   3749 Elmington Drive, (PA)

3. *Lt. James Reichelder, Sr.*
   Court Clerk E. Gradefelder
   Witness: Gregory F. Boulder
   Evidence Rep. 3917: 2 Folio
   F: 2857930-892 (Series A-B)

4. Services Report K-9721979
   Court Clerk H. **Womanski**
   JHO James Williamson
   Seq. (TA-1 - 4893234)
   Wasserman and Brystol

5. Brooklyn, NY 11246-2019
   JHO F. Schneider-Hamilton
   783-07-2203 and 978-4
   Rooms (307), (448)
   Surrogates Procedures 2020

---

1. Hazton, Spitzdorf, & Hines
   Surrogates Court Pub. 18K
   2852 Mahasset, Suite 3A-4
   New York, NY 10029-2568
   ID #: 486759-2019 (D)

2. 797554-437958 KCV-25
   Chambers 8635, 9829, 1035
   CPLR 1002 and CPL 3472 g)
   2/29/18, 4/12/20, 3/7/21
   3749 El**mimgt**on Drive, (PA)

3. Lt. James Reichelder, Sr.
   Court Clerk E. Gradefelder
   Witness: Gregory F. Boulder
   Evidence Rep. 3917: 2 Folio
   F: 2857930-892 (Series A-B)

4. Services Report K-9721979
   Court Clerk H. **Womensky**
   JHO James Williamson
   Seq. (TA-1 - 4893234)
   Wasserman and Brystol

5. Brooklyn, NY 11246-2019
   JHO F. Schneider-Hamilton
   738-07- 2203 and 978-4
   Rooms (307), (448)
   Surrogates Procedures 2020

Explanations:

1. C (only the first and third sets are exactly alike)
The ID#: in the second set has a "2" instead of a "5"

2. B (only the first and second sets are exactly alike)
"Elmington" in set 3 is spelled "Elmi**m**gton", with an "m" instead of an "n".

3. A (all three sets are exactly alike)

All 3 sets are exactly alike because the use of different fonts (Example: bold, *italics*, ALL CAPITALS, etc.) does <u>not</u> change the information (which is the only thing you are comparing.) Court Officers handle many different types of papers every day (handwritten, typed, printed, etc.). The <u>presentation</u> may be different, but this does <u>not</u> change the <u>information</u>.

4. D (none of the three sets are exactly alike)
"Womenski" (set 1) is spelled "Wom**a**nski" in set 2 and Women**sky**" in set 3.

5. B (only the first and second sets are exactly alike)
"783" in sets 1 and 2 is "**738**" in set 3

Court Officer New York State (NYS Court Officer Trainee)

Instructions: Questions 6-10 (below) consist of three sets of information. Compare the information in each set and mark your answer sheet, as follows:

Mark: Choice A if none of the three sets are exactly alike
        Choice B if only the first and third sets are exactly alike
        Choice C if only the first and second sets are exactly alike
        Choice D if all of the three sets are exactly alike.

6. IOD: 9/22/19, 12/22/19
   Queens, NY 11378-3217
   Seq. Ref.: O-719-71335
   Leighton Burrows (Oneida)
   354 Kingsway St., 3rd floor

6. IOD: 9/22/19, 12/22/19
   Queens, NY 11373-3217
   Seq. Ref.: O-719-71335
   Leighton Burrows (Oneida)
   354 Kingsway St., 3rd floor

6. IOD: 9/22/19, 12/22/19
   Queens, NY 11378-3217
   Seq. Ref.: O-719-71355
   Lieghton Burrows (Oneida)
   354 Kingsway St., 3rd floor

7. CPL Section 5029(d) (2019)
   Court Officer Underwood
   ID # 8649111567-720 (2017)
   1892-A Vanderbilt Parkway
   Martin Jefkowitz, ID: G-7298

7. CPL Section 5029(d) (2019)
   Court Officer Underwood
   ID # 8649111567-720 (2017)
   1892-A Vanderbilt Parkway
   Martin Jefkowitz, ID: G-7298

7. CPL Section 5029(d) (2019)
   Court Officer Underwood
   ID # 8649111567-720 (2017)
   1892-A Vanderbilt Parkway
   Martin Jefkowitz, ID: G-7298

8. 825 N. Cumberland, NJ
   Controlled substance section
   Judge Elmor Washington
   Req. #: 567/2019 (Warner)
   Sealed file S:48956/2018

8. 825 N. Cumberland, NJ
   Controlled substance section
   Judge Elmor Washington
   Req. #: 567/2019 (Warner)
   Sealed file S:48956/2018

8. 825 N. Cumberland, NJ
   Controlled substance section
   Judge Elmor Washington
   Req. #: 567/2019 (Warner)
   Sealed file F:48956/2018

9. Kirschner, Richard (Supreme)
   (869) 592-8539 (8 a.m.)
   Holmesville, NY, 10786-9585
   457-29 Montana Boulevard
   Examiner Barry Johnson

9. Kirschner, Richard (Supreme)
   (869) 592-8539 (8 a.m.)
   Homesville, NY, 10786-9585
   457-29 Montana Boulevard
   Examiner Barry Johnson

9. Kirschner, Richard (Supreme)
   (869) 592-8539 (8 a.m.)
   Holmesville, NY, 10786-9585
   457-29 Montana Boulevard
   Examiner Barry Johnson

10. Sleepy Hollow, NY 16739
   Corvana Road (17682)
   Justice Peter Wilkins-Proctor
   ID: 867219802-76509396
   Reg. 2019/C-459 (d) and (e)

10. Sleepy Hollow, NY 16739
   Corvana Road (17682)
   Justice Peter Wilkins-Proctor
   ID: 867219802-76509396
   Reg. 2019/C-459 (d) and (e)

10. Sleepy Hollow, NY 16739
   Corvana Road (17682)
   Justice Peter Wilkins-Proctor
   ID: 867219802-76509396
   Reg. 2019/C-459 (d) and (e)

Answer Sheet

6.A◯ B◯ C◯ D◯
7.A◯ B◯ C◯ D◯
8.A◯ B◯ C◯ D◯
9.A◯ B◯ C◯ D◯
10.A◯ B◯ C◯ D◯

Answers are on next page.

There is something in the above 5 questions that makes many candidates answer incorrectly. Can you tell what that is?

!

Answers 6-10

6. IOD: 9/22/19, 12/22/19
   Queens, NY 11378-3217
   Seq. Ref.: O-719-71335
   Leighton Burrows (Oneida)
   354 Kingsway St., 3rd floor

6. IOD: 9/22/19, 12/22/19
   Queens, NY 11**73**-3217
   Seq. Ref.: O-719-71335
   Leighton Burrows (Oneida)
   354 Kingsway St., 3rd floor

6. IOD: 9/22/19, 12/22/19
   Queens, NY 11378-3217
   Seq. Ref.: O-719-713**55**
   L**ie**ghton Burrows (Oneida)
   354 Kingsway St., 3rd floor

7. CPL Section 5029(d) (2019)
   Court Officer Underwood
   ID # 8649111567-720 (2017)
   1892-A Vanderbilt Parkway
   Martin Jefkowitz, ID: G-7298

7. CPL Section 5029(d) (2019)
   Court Officer Underwood
   ID # 8649111567-720 (2017)
   1892-A Vanderbilt Parkway
   Martin Jefkowitz, ID: G-7298

7. CPL Section 5029(d) (2019)
   Court Officer Underwood
   ID # 8649111567-720 (2017)
   1892-A Vanderbilt Parkway
   Martin Jefkowitz, ID: G-7298

8. 825 N. Cumberland, NJ
   Controlled substance section
   Judge Elmor Washington
   Req. #: 567/2019 (Warner)
   Sealed file S:48956/2018

8. 825 N. Cumberland, NJ
   Controlled substance section
   Judge Elmor Washington
   Req. #: 567/2019 (Warner)
   Sealed file S:48956/2018

8. 825 N. Cumberland, NJ
   Controlled substance section
   Judge Elmor Washington
   Req. #: 567/2019 (Warner)
   Sealed file **F:**48956/2018

9. Kirschner, Richard (Supreme)
   (869) 592-8539 (8 a.m.)
   Holmesville, NY, 10786-9585
   457-29 Montana Boulevard
   Examiner Barry Johnson

9. Kirschner, Richard (Supreme)
   (869) 592-8539 (8 a.m.)
   Homesville, NY, 10786-9585
   457-29 Montana Boulevard
   Examiner Barry Johnson

9. Kirschner, Richard (Supreme)
   (869) 592-8539 (8 a.m.)
   Holmesville, NY, 10786-9585
   457-29 Montana Boulevard
   Examiner Barry Johnson

10. Sleepy Hollow, NY 16739
    Corvana Road (17682)
    Justice Peter Wilkins-Proctor
    ID: 867219802-76509396
    Reg. 2019/C-459 (d) and (e)

10. *Sleepy Hollow, NY 16739*
    Corvana Road (17682)
    Justice Peter Wilkins-Proctor
    ID: 867219802-76509396
    Reg. 2019/C-459 (d) and (e)

10. Sleepy Hollow, NY 16739
    Corvana Road (17682)
    Justice Peter Wilkins-Proctor
    ID: 867219802-76509396
    Reg. 2019/C-459 (d) and (e)

Explanations:

NOTE THAT THE ANSWER CHOICES FOR QUESTIONS 6-10 (A, B, C, D) ARE **DIFFERENT** FROM THE ANSWER CHOICES FOR QUESTIONS 1-5. ON THE ACTUAL TEST YOU MAY BE ASKED TO ANSWER 10 QUESTIONS (1-5 on one page and 6-10 ON THE FOLLOWING PAGE. **THE INSTRUCTIONS AT THE TOP OF EACH PAGE MAY BE THE SAME OR THEY MAY BE DIFFERENT.**

6. A (none of the three sets are exactly alike)

Seq. Ref.: O-719-71335	Seq. Ref.: O-719-71335	Seq. Ref.: O-719-713**55**
Queens, NY 11378-3217	Queens, NY 113**73**-3217	Queens, NY 11378-3217
Leighton Burrows (Oneida)	Leighton Burrows (Oneida)	L**ie**ghton Burrows (Oneida)

7. D (all of the three sets are exactly alike)

8. C (only the first and second sets are exactly alike)

| Sealed file S:48956/2018 | Sealed file S:48956/2018 | Sealed file **F:**48956/2018 |

9. B (only the first and third sets are exactly alike)

| Holmesville, NY, 10786-9585 | **Home**sville, NY, 10786-9585 | Holmesville, NY, 10786-9585 |

10. D (all of the three sets are exactly alike) (The bold and italic fonts do **not** change the information!)

Exercise 1 Instructions: Questions 1-5 (below) consist of three sets of information. Compare the information in each set and mark your answer sheet, as follows:

Mark: Choice A if all three sets are exactly alike

Choice B if none of the three sets are exactly alike

Choice C if only the second and third sets are exactly alike

Choice D if only the first and second sets are exactly alike

1. Bronx, NY 11246-10457
   Judge A. Vladimer Kurochov
   452-05-2592 (Sept. 26, 2019)
   Rooms (326), (349), (728)
   Criminal Procedure 280(f)

2. POS: 4/28/18, 11/27/19
   Queens, NY 11425-4238
   Seq. Ref.: B-8943-6837525
   Bryan Marinowski (Oswego)
   124 86th St., 3rd and 4th flrs.

3. CPLR Sect. 5024(c) (2018)
   Court Officer Jay Maldonado
   ID # 3792414937-525 (2018)
   3291-A Jefferson Boulevard
   Charles James Huang,G-798

4. 9325 S. Wallenfield, NY
   Support collection unit 7-NYC
   Judge Kilmer Cheng, Senior
   Req. #: 65398959 (Haskins)
   Sealed file W:3379183683

5. Davidson, Francisco (Civil)
   (365) 694-8469 (9 a.m.)
   Dellaford, NY, 10384-5515
   672-23 Dakota Parkway
   Magistrate Timothy Biesdorf

1. Bronx, NY 11246-10457
   Judge A. Vladimer Kurochov
   452-05-2595 (Sept. 26, 2019)
   Rooms (326), (349), (728)
   Criminal Procedure 280(f)

2. POS: 4/28/18, 11/27/19
   Queens, NY 11425-4238
   Seq. Ref.: B-8943-6837525
   Bryan Marinowski (Oswego)
   124 86th St., 3rd and 4th flrs.

3. CPLR Sect. 5024(e) (2018)
   Court Officer Jay Maldonado
   ID # 3792414937-525 (2018)
   3291-A Jefferson Boulevard
   Charles James Huang,G-798

4. 9325 S. Wallenfield, NY
   Support collection unit 7-NYC
   Judge Kilmer Chang, Senior
   Req. #: 65398959 (Haskins)
   Sealed file W:3379183683

5. Davidson, Francisco (Civil)
   (365) 694-8469 (9 a.m.)
   Dellaford, NY, 10384-5515
   672-23 Dakota Parkway
   Magistrate Timothy Biesdorf

1. Bronx, NY 11246-10457
   Judge A. Vladimer Kurockov
   452-05-2592 (Sept. 26, 2019)
   Rooms (326), (349), (728)
   Criminal Procedure 280(f)

2. POS: 4/28/18, 11/27/19
   Queens, NY 11425-4238
   Seq. Ref.: B-8943-6837525
   Bryan Marinouski (Oswego)
   124 86th St., 3rd and 4th flrs.

3. CPLR Sect. 5024(e) (2018)
   Court Officer Jay Maldonado
   ID # 3792414937-525 (2018)
   3291-A Jefferson Boulevard
   Charles James Huang,G-798

4. 9325 S. Wallenfield, NY
   Support collection unit 7-NYC
   Judge Kilmer Chang, Senior
   Req. #: 65398959 (Haskins)
   Sealed file W:3379183683

5. Davidson, Francisco (Civil)
   (365) 694-8469 (9 a.m.)
   Dellaford, NY, 10384-5515
   672-23 Dakota Parkway
   Magistrate Timothy Beisdorf

Continue to the next page and answer questions 6-10.

Instructions; Questions 6-10 (below) consist of three sets of information. Compare the information in each set and mark your answer sheet, as follows:

Mark: Choice A if all three sets are exactly alike

        Choice B if none of the three sets are exactly alike.

        Choice C if only the second and third sets are exactly alike

        Choice D if only the first and second sets are exactly alike

6. Filmor Junction, NY 16334
Bryant Highway (East 13652)
Justice Frank S. Cupertino
ID: 486342352-45269936
Reg. 2019/S-255 (w) and (y)

6. Filmor Junction, NY 16334
Bryant Highway (East 13652)
Justice Frank S. Cupertino
ID: 486342352-45269936
Reg. 2019/S-255 (w) and (y)

6. Filmor Junction, NY 16334
Bryant Highway (East 13652)
Justice Frank S. Cupertino
ID: 486342352-45269936
Reg. 2019/S-255 (w) and (y)

7. Gurgoen, Jenkins, Feinstein
Civil Procedures and Rules
32-149 Lamport Boulevard
Albany, NY 12238-3892
Ref. #: 4895259-1673 (A)

7. Gurgoen, Jenkins, Feinstein
Civil Procedures and Rules
32-149 Lamports Boulevard
Albany, NY 12238-3892
Ref. #: 4895259-1673 (A)

7. Gurgoen, Jenkins, Feinstein
Civil Procedures and Rules
32-149 Lamports Boulevard
Albany, NY 12238-3892
Ref. #: 4895259-1673 (A)

8. 50983376-891490 BAR-259
Store Rms. 5639, 2845, 2027
SCPA 201(b) and CPL 244(g)
8/25/16, 7/11/19, 8/7/22
2728 Brighton Avenue, (CT)

8. 50983376-891490 BAR-259
Store Rms. 5639, 2845, 2027
SCPA 201(b) and CPL 244(g)
8/25/16, 7/11/19, 8/7/22
2728 Brighton Avenue, (CT)

8. 5098376-891490 BAR-259
Store Rms. 5639, 2845, 2027
SCPA 201(b) and CPL 244(g)
8/25/16, 7/11/19, 8/7/22
2728 Brighton Avenue, (CT)

9. Sgt. Winston Ramirez, Jr.
Ct. Off. Sgt. Brandon Helps
Witness: Marina Elsa Chan
Police Report 5937: 8 Series
H: 3698970-386 (Series D-F)

9. Sgt. Winston Ramirez, Jr.
Ct. Off. Sgt. Brandon Helps
Witness: Marina Elsa Chan
Police Report 5937: 8 Series
H: 3693970-386 (Series D-F)

9. Sgt. Winston Ramirez, Jr.
Ct. Off. Sgt. Brandon Helps
Witness: Marina Elsa Chan
Police Report 5937: 8 Series
H: 3693970-386 (Series D-F)

10. Services Report L-42689659
Court Reporter Z. Kuminetis
Magistrate Michael Ellison
Seq. (BKS 3 - 98742384564)
Mohamed Green: 73975924

10. Services Report L-42689659
Court Reporter Z. Kuminetis
Magistrate Michael Ellison
Seq. (BKS 8 - 98742384564)
Mohamed Green: 73975924

10. Services Report L-42689659
Court Reporter Z. Kuminetis
Magistrate Michael Ellison
Seq. (BKS 3 - 98745384564)
Mohamed Green: 73975924

Answers for 1-10 are on the following page.

Answers for questions 1-10 on the preceding two pages:

Did you check whether there were any differences in the instructions for questions 1-5 and 6-10?

In this case, the instructions were <u>the same</u>.

1. B (none of the three sets are exactly alike)

Judge A. Vladimer Kurochov	Judge A. Vladimer Kurochov	Judge A. Vladimer Kuro**ckov**
452-05-2592 (Sept. 26, 2019)	452-05-25**95** (Sept. 26, 2019)	452-05-2592 (Sept. 26, 2019)

2. D (only the first and second sets are exactly alike)

Bryan Marinowski (Oswego)	Bryan Marinowski (Oswego)	Bryan Marin**ousk**i (Oswego)

3. C (only the second and third sets are exactly alike)

CPLR Sect. 5024**(c)** (2018)	CPLR Sect. 5024(e) (2018)	CPLR Sect. 5024(e) (2018)

4. C (only the second and third sets are exactly alike

Judge Kilmer C**hen**g, Senior	Judge Kilmer Chang, Senior	Judge Kilmer Chang, Senior

5. D (only the first and second sets are exactly alike)

Magistrate Timothy Biesdorf	Magistrate Timothy Biesdorf	Magistrate Timothy B**eis**dorf

6. A (all three sets are exactly alike)

7. C (only the second and third sets are exactly alike)

32-149 Lamp**ort** Boulevard	32-149 Lamports Boulevard	32-149 Lamports Boulevard

8. D (only the first and second sets are exactly alike)

50983376-891490 BAR-259	50983376-891490 BAR-259	5098**376**-891490 BAR-259

9. C (only the second and third sets are exactly alike)

H: 3**6989**70-386 (Series D-F)	H: 3693970-386 (Series D-F)	H: 3693970-386 (Series D-F)

10. B (if none of the three sets are exactly alike)

Seq. (BKS 3 - 98742384564)	Seq. (BK**S 8** - 98742384564)	Seq. (BKS 3 - 987**4538**4564)

TYPES OF DIFFERENCES

Letters omitted (Bakers and Baker)
Letters added (Anabelle and Annabelle)
Letters inverted (Feinberg and Fienberg)
Numbers inverted (1489 and 1498)
Numbers omitted (11117845 and 1117845)
Numbers added (872587 and 8722587)

Court Officer New York State (NYS Court Officer-Trainee)

Exercise 2 Instructions: Questions 1-5 (below) consist of three sets of information. Compare the information in each set and mark your answer sheet, as follows:

A. Only the second and third sets are exactly alike
B. Only the first and second sets are exactly alike
C. None of the sets are exactly alike
D. All three sets are exactly alike

1. 725225963827-3876
   Centre Street, NY
   Jimmy-Lee Sanders
   Attempted Mischief (B)
   Horowitz, Nathaniel

2. 497374-438768 KCV-97
   Rooms 3625, 4852, 8032
   SCPA 902 and CPL 2482
   3/25/19, 5/16/20, 8/3/20
   2747 Vandam Drive, (NY)

3. Sgt. Kyle Beinman, Sr.
   Court Int. S. Morales, Sn.
   Witness: Thomas F. Nunez
   SS Report 2917: (2865347)
   K: 2697950-292 (Series N-P)

4. Serv. Report SDK-3801277
   Senior Court Clerk Berinski
   JHO Giovanni Verazano
   Seq. (LDA-1 - 7869764)
   Cummings and Lafauci

5. Bronx, NY 11246-9671
   JHO Harold Jefferson, Jr.
   482-17-5203 and 288-4
   Rooms (607-A), (929 -B)
   Surrogates Court (NY)

---

1. 725225963827-3876
   Centre Street, NY
   Jimmy-Lee Sanders
   Attempted Mischief (B)
   Horowitz, Nathaniel

2. 497374-438768 KCV-97
   Rooms 3625, 4822, 8032
   SCPA 902 and CPL 2482
   3/25/19, 5/16/20, 8/3/20
   2747 Vandam Drive, (NY)

3. Sgt. Kyle Beinman, Sr.
   Court Int. S. Morales, Sn.
   Witness: Thomas F. Nunez
   SS Report 2917: (2865347)
   K: 2697950-292 (Series N-P)

4. Serv. Report SDK-3801277
   Senior Court Clerk Berinski
   JHO Giovanni Verrazano
   Seq. (LDA-1 - 7869764)
   Cummings and Lafauci

5. Bronx, NY 11246-9671
   JHO Harold Jefferson, Jr.
   482-17-5203 and 288-4
   Rooms (607-A), (929 -B)
   Surrogates Court (NY)

---

1. 725225963827-3876
   Centre Street, NY
   Jimmy-Lee Sanders
   Attempted Mischief (B)
   Horovitz, Nathaniel

2. 497374-438763 KCV-97
   Rooms 3625, 4822, 8032
   SCPA 902 and CPL 2482
   3/25/19, 5/16/20, 8/3/20
   2747 Vandam Drive, (NY)

3. K: 2697950-292 (Series N-P)
   SS Report 2917: (2865347)
   Witness: Thomas F. Nunez
   Court Int. S. Morales, Sn.
   Sgt. Kyle Beinman, Sr.

4. Serv. Report SDK-3801277
   Senior Court Clerk Berinski
   JHO Giovanni Verrazano
   Seq. (LDA-1 - 7869764)
   Cummings and Lafauci

5. Bronx, NY 11246-9671
   JHO Harold Jeferson, Jr.
   482-17-5203 and 288-4
   Rooms (607-A), (929 -B)
   Surrogates Court (NY)

Continue to the next page and answer questions 6-10.

Court Officer New York State (NYS Court Officer-Trainee)

Instructions: Questions 6-10 (below) consist of three sets of information. Compare the information in each set and mark your answer sheet, as follows:
A. Only the first and second sets are exactly alike.
B. Only the second and third sets are exactly alike.
C. None of the three sets are exactly alike.
D. All three sets are exactly alike.

6. PQR: 5/29/18, 11/79/19
   New York, NY 11338-2257
   Seq. Ref.: L-375-4983297
   William Scatters (Oswego)
   852 Queens Village, 2 fl.

6. PQR: 5/29/18, 11/79/19
   New York, NY 11338-2257
   Seq. Ref.: L-375-4983297
   William Scatters (Oswego)
   852 Queens Village, 2 fl.

6. PQR: 5/29/18, 11/79/19
   New York, NY 11338-2257
   Seq. Ref.: L-375-4983597
   William Scatters (Oswego)
   852 Queens Village, 2 fl.

7. SCPA Section 2049(e) (2018)
   Court Officer Rickerman
   ID # 3429177561-120 (2018)
   1289-B Vinniker Parkway
   Marietta Keilman, JHO

7. SCPA Section 2049(c) (2018)
   Court Officer Rickerman
   ID # 3429177561-120 (2018)
   1289-B Vinniker Parkway
   Marietta Keilman, JHO

7. SCPA Section 2049(e) (2013)
   Court Officer Rickerman
   ID # 3429177561-120 (2018)
   1289-B Vinniker Parkway
   Marietta Keilman, JHO

8. 329 S. Vineland, NJ
   Substance abuse section
   Judge Samuel H. Lincoln
   Req. #: 525/2018 (Bailey)
   Sealed file M:34378/2019

8. 329 S. Vineland, NJ
   Substance abuse section
   Judge Samuel H. Lincoln
   Req. #: 525/2018 (Bailey)
   Sealed file M:34378/2019

8. 329 S. Vineland, NJ
   Substance abuse section
   Judge Samuel H. Lincoln
   Req. #: 525/2018 (Baily)
   Sealed file M:34378/2019

9. Hardy, Harry (Supreme Civil)
   2869) 582-2769 (9 a.m.)
   Outerbank, NY, 10736-2584
   257-94 Nebraska Boulevard
   Support Examiner Chanks

9. Hardy, Harry (Supreme Civil)
   2869) 582-2769 (9 a.m.)
   Outerbanks, NY, 10736-2584
   257-94 Nebraska Boulevard
   Support Examiner Chanks

9. Hardy, Harry (Supreme Civil)
   2869) 582-2769 (9 a.m.)
   Outerbanks, NY, 10736-2584
   257-94 Nebraska Boulevard
   Support Examiner Chanks

10. Widerville, NY 13749-8762
    Fayetteville Road (12662)
    Justice Anthony L. Frances
    ID: 837919231-73809327
    Reg. 2018/C-253 (d) and (f)

10. Widerville, NY 13749-8762
    Fayetteville Road (12662)
    Justice Anthony L. Francis
    ID: 837919231-73809327
    Reg. 2018/C-253 (d) and (f)

10. Widerville, NY 13749-8762
    Fayetteville Road (12662)
    Justice Anthony L. Francis
    ID: 837919231-73809327
    Reg. 2018/C-253 (d) and (f)

Answers for 1-10 are on the following page.

Answers for questions 1-10 on the preceding pages:

Did you check whether there were any differences in the instruction for questions 1-5 and 6-10?

In this case, the instructions were <u>different</u>.

1. B (Only the first and second sets are exactly alike)

Horowitz, Nathaniel   Horowitz, Nathaniel   Hor**ovit**z, Nathaniel

2. C (None of the sets are exactly alike)

497374-438768 KCV-97   497374-438768 KCV-97   497374-438**763** KCV-97

Rooms 3625, 4**852**, 8032   Rooms 3625, 4822, 8032   Rooms 3625, 4822, 8032

3. D (All three sets are exactly alike) Note: If the information in the three sets is in a <u>different order</u>, the difference in the order does **NOT** make a difference in the information of the sets.

4. A (Only the second and third sets are exactly alike)

JHO Giovanni **Vera**zano   JHO Giovanni Verrazano   JHO Giovanni Verrazano

5. B (Only the first and second sets are exactly alike)

JHO Harold Jefferson, Jr.   JHO Harold Jefferson, Jr.   JHO Harold **Jefer**son, Jr.

6. A (Only the first and second sets are exactly alike)

Seq. Ref.: L-375-4983297   Seq. Ref.: L-375-4983297   Seq. Ref.: L-375-498**3597**

7. C (None of the sets are exactly alike)

SCPA Section 2049(e) (2018)   SCPA Section 20**49(c)** (2018)   SCPA Section 2049(e) **(2013)**

8. A (Only the first and second sets are exactly alike)

Req. #: 525/2018 (Bailey)   Req. #: 525/2018 (Bailey)   Req. #: 525/2018 **(Baily)**

9. B (Only the second and third sets are exactly alike)

Outer**bank,** NY, 10736-2584   Outerbanks, NY, 10736-2584   Outerbanks, NY, 10736-2584

10. B (Only the second and third sets are exactly alike)

Justice Anthony L. Fran**ces**   Justice Anthony L. Francis   Justice Anthony L. Francis

HINT!

If you finish the test early, it might be a good idea to double-check your answers for this section of the test - especially those questions where you did not find any differences among the three groups of information.

Exercise 3 Instructions: Questions 1-5 (below) consist of three sets of information. Compare the information in each set and mark your answer sheet, as follows:

Mark: Choice A if all three sets are exactly alike
Choice B if none of the three sets are exactly alike
Choice C if only the first and second sets are exactly alike
Choice D if only the second and third sets are exactly alike

1. Report ALG -48062372
   Junior Court Asst. Borman
   Int. Albert Martinnoff
   SQL. (MFH-3 - 58697163)
   Parsons and Keirfman
	1. Report ALG -48062372
	   Junior Court Asst. Borman
	   Int. Albert Martinnoff
	   SQL. (MFH-3 - 58697163)
	   Parsons and Keirfman
		1. Report ALG -48062372
		   Junior Court Asst. Borman
		   Int. Albert Martinoff
		   SQL. (MFH-3 - 58697163)
		   Parsons and Keirfman

2. 395384-428467 KCV-98
   Floors: Mezz., 3, 6, 8, 9
   EPTL 301 and FCA 3453
   6/30/19, 8/19/17, 5/6/16
   5728 Firsten Circle N.
	2. 395384-428467 KCV-98
	   Floors: Mezz., 3, 6, 8, 9
	   EPTL 301 and FCA 3453
	   6/30/19, 8/19/17, 5/6/16
	   5728 Firsten Circle N.
		2. 395384-428467 KCV-98
		   Floors: Mezz., 3, 6, 8, 9
		   EPTL 301 and FCA 3453
		   6/30/19, 8/19/17, 5/6/16
		   5728 Firsten Circle N.

3. Master Ben Bright, Sr..
   Civil Court Int. A. Miranda
   Witness: George Madison
   SS Report 3952: (3668343)
   R: 3695952-292 (Series W-X)
	3. Master Ben Bright, Sr.
	   Civil Court Int. A. Miranda
	   Witness: George Madison
	   SS Report 3955: (3668343)
	   R: 3695952-292 (Series W-X)
		3. Master Ben Bright, Sr.
		   Civil Court Int. A. Miranda
		   Witness: George Madison
		   SS Report 3955: (3668343)
		   R: 3695952-292 (Series W-X)

4. Queens, NY 11343-9572
   JHO Harold Jefferson, Jr.
   5823, 5887, 5924, 6075
   Rooms (307-C), (722 -D)
   Court of Claims, (NY)
	4. Queens, NY 11343-9572
	   JHO Harold Jefferson, Jr.
	   5823, 5887, 5924, 6072
	   Rooms (307-C), (722 -D)
	   Court of Claims, (NY)
		4. Queens, NY 11343-9572
		   JHO Harold Jeferson, Jr.
		   5823, 5887, 5924, 6075
		   Rooms (307-C), (722 -D)
		   Court of Claims, (NY)

5. 425925163522-4852
   Fulton Street, Brooklyn
   James Harris Modina
   PL 5502 (Sect. 34 - 42)
   Horowitz, Nathaniel
	5. 425925163522-4852
	   Fulton Street, Brooklyn
	   James Harris Modina
	   PL 5502 (Sect. 34 - 42)
	   Horowitz, Nathaniel
		5. 425925163522-4852
		   Fulton Street, Brooklyn
		   James Harris Modina
		   PL 5502 (Sect. 34 - 42)
		   Horowitz, Nathaniel

Continue to the next page and answer questions 6-10.

Exercise 3 Instructions: Questions 6-10 (below) consist of three sets of information. Compare the information in each set and mark your answer sheet, as follows:

Mark: Choice A if all three sets are exactly alike

Choice B if only the second and third sets are exactly alike

Choice C if none of the three sets are exactly alike

Choice D if only the first and second sets are exactly alike

6. Serv. Report ASK-3608227 ACC John F. McKelly Judge Martha G. Quinones File Storage AD38795 Ingram, Kerner and Lohman	6. Serv. Report ASK-3608227 ACC John F. McKelly Judge Martha G. Quinones File Storage AD38795 Ingram, Kerner and Lohman	6. Serv. Report ASK-3608227 ACC John F. McKelly Judge Martha G. Quinones File Storage AD38795 Ingram, Kerner and Lorman
7. 1872 Ryder Street, Queens Parts 18C, 22F, 31D, 32A FCA 412: Support NYS 5/28/18, 4/18/19, 4/2/19 2243 Madison Avenue (NY)	7. 1872 Ryder Street, Queens Parts 18C, 22F, 31D, 32A FCA 412: Support NYS 5/28/18, 4/13/19, 4/2/19 2243 Madison Avenue (NY)	7. 1872 Ryder Street, Queens Parts 18C, 22F, 31D, 32A FCA 412: Support NYS 5/28/18, 4/13/19, 4/2/19 2243 Madison Avenue (NY)
8. PFC Anita Johnson, Sr. Court Officer-Trainee Jones Witness: Barbara M. Belos IR Report 3934: (5875942) L: 3694958-232 (Series DPM)	8. PFC Anita Johnson, Sr. Court Officer-Trainee Jones Witness: Barbara M. Bellos IR Report 3934: (5875942) L: 3694958-232 (Series DPM)	8. PFC Annita Johnson, Sr. Court Officer-Trainee Jones Witness: Barbara M. Bellos IR Report 3934: (5875942) L: 3694958-232 (Series DPM)
9. Richmond County, NY Spec. Diana F. Rodriguez 385-47-4202 and 375-3 Rooms (503-b), (916 -d) County Court, Nassau (NY)	9. Richmond County, NY Spec. Diana F. Rodriguez 385-47-4202 and 375-3 Rooms (503-b), (916 -d) County Court, Nassau (NY)	9. Richmond County, NY Spec. Diana F. Rodriguez 385-47-4202 and 375-3 Rooms (503-b), (916 -b) County Court, Nassau (NY)
10. 225825263523-2842 Eastern Parkway, NY Jeffry M. Hamilton, Sr. Reckless Endangerment Ludwig and Martello, PC	10. 225825263523-2842 Eastern Parkway, NY Jeffry M. Hamilton, Sr. Reckless Endangerment Ludwig and Martello, PC	10. 225825263523-2842 Eastern Parkway, NY Jeffry M. Hamilton, Sr. Reckless Endangerment Ludwig and Marteillo, PC

Continue to the next page and answer questions 11-15.

Exercise 3 Instructions: Questions 11-15 (below) consist of three sets of information. Compare the information in each set and mark your answer sheet, as follows:

Mark: Choice A if all three sets are exactly alike

        Choice B if none of the three sets are exactly alike

        Choice C if only the first and second sets are exactly alike

        Choice D if only the second and third sets are exactly alike

11. September 28, 2019: 9:AM
    Sections 25D, 25A, and 26F
    4593-28 East 16th Street
    May 24, 2019: Building 7
    9378 Rockaway Street, NY
	11. September 28, 2019: 9:AM
	    Sections 25D, 25A, and 26F
	    4593-28 East 16th Street
	    May 24, 2019: Building 7
	    9378 Rockaway Street, NY
		11. September 28, 2019: 9:AM
		    Sections 25D, 25A, and 26F
		    4593-28 East 16th Street
		    May 24, 2019: Building 7
		    9373 Rockaway Street, NY

12. CR Brenda Williams
    Court Int. A. Miller: Sect 5
    Expert Witness F. James
    Report 2019: 6-22 Cat. 7
    5698953-21217 (Series O)
	12. CR Brenda Williams
	    Court Int. A. Miller: Sect 5
	    Expert Witness F. James
	    Report 2019: 6-22 Cat. 7
	    5698953-21217 (Series Q)
		12. CR Brenda Williams
		    Court Int. A. Miller: Sect 5
		    Expert Witness F. James
		    Report 2019: 6-22 Cat. 7
		    5698953-21217 (Series Q)

13. SI, NY 10414-2972
    Major James B. Holliman
    287-27-2243 and 184-9
    Rooms (304-B), (823 -C)
    Criminal Supreme Court (NY)
	13. SI, NY 10414-2972
	    Major James B. Holliman
	    287-27-2243 and 184-9
	    Rooms (304-B), (823 -C)
	    Criminal Supreme Court (NY)
		13. SI, NY 10414-2972
		    Major James B. Holliman
		    287-27-2243 and 184-9
		    Rooms (304-B), (823 -C)
		    Criminal Supreme Court (NY)

14. 224215943924-2851
    Canal and Beeker Streets
    Carlos Francisco Morales
    Felonies and Misdemeanors
    Winneg and Esposito, LLC
	14. 224215943924-2851
	    Canal and Beeker Streets
	    Carlos Francisco Morales
	    Felonies and Misdemeanors
	    Winneg and Esposito, LLC
		14. 224215943924-2857
		    Canal and Beeker Streets
		    Carlos Francisco Morales
		    Felonies and Misdemeanors
		    Winneg and Esposito, LLC

15. Yearly Summary G-6849
    Court Asst. Elen Barrillo
    JHO Nathaniel Bannister
    Seq. (SDG-2 - 48793642
    Finnerman and Carlton
	15. Yearly Summary G-6849
	    Court Asst. Elen Barillo
	    JHO Nathaniel Bannister
	    Seq. (SDG-2 - 48793642
	    Finnerman and Carlton
		15. Yearly Summary G-6849
		    Court Asst. Elen Barillo
		    JHO Nathaniel Bannister
		    Seq. (SDG-2 - 48793642
		    Finnerman and Carlton

Answers 1-15 are on the following page.

Exercise 3 Answers:

1. Choice C if only the first and second sets are exactly alike

Int. Albert Martinnoff   Int. Albert Martinnoff   Int. Albert Mart**inoff**

2. Choice A if all three sets are exactly alike

3. Choice D if only the second and third sets are exactly alike

SS Report 39**52**: (3668343)   SS Report 3955: (3668343)   SS Report 3955: (3668343)

4. Choice B if none of the three sets are exactly alike

JHO Harold Jefferson, Jr.   JHO Harold Jefferson, Jr.   JHO Harold **Jefer**son, Jr.
5823, 5887, 5924, 6075   5823, 5887, 5924, **6072**   5823, 5887, 5924, 6075

5. Choice A if all three sets are exactly alike

6. Choice D if only the first and second sets are exactly alike

Ingram, Kerner and Lohman   Ingram, Kerner and Lohman   Ingram, Kerner and **Lorm**an

7. Choice B if only the second and third sets are exactly alike

5/28/18, 4/**18**/19, 4/2/19   5/28/18, 4/13/19, 4/2/19   5/28/18, 4/13/19, 4/2/19

8. Choice C if none of the three sets are exactly alike

PFC Anita Johnson, Sr.   PFC Anita Johnson, Sr.   PFC **Annita** Johnson, Sr.
Witness: Barbara M. **Belos**   Witness: Barbara M. Bellos   Witness: Barbara M. Bellos

9. Choice D if only the first and second sets are exactly alike

Rooms (503-b), (916 -d)   Rooms (503-b), (916 -d)   Rooms (503-b), (916 **-b)**

10. Choice D if only the first and second sets are exactly alike

Ludwig and Martello, PC   Ludwig and Martello, PC   Ludwig and Ma**rteill**o, PC

11. Choice C if only the first and second sets are exactly alike

9378 Rockaway Street, NY   9378 Rockaway Street, NY   **9373** Rockaway Street, NY

12. Choice D if only the second and third sets are exactly alike

5698953-21217 **(Series O)**   5698953-21217 (Series Q) 5698953-21217 (Series Q)

13. Choice A if all three sets are exactly alike

14. Choice C if only the first and second sets are exactly alike

224215943924-2851   224215943924-2851   224215943924-**2857**

15. Choice D if only the second and third sets are exactly alike

Court Asst. Elen B**arrill**o   Court Asst. Elen Barillo   Court Asst. Elen Barrillo

CHAPTER 4: Reading and Understanding Written Material

Format A: Understanding the content of a written passage

This type of question tests your ability to understand the content of a document. This ability is important to Court Officers because they come in contact with many types of papers every day - from legal papers and other materials received from litigants to court directives, policies, and actual laws.

The following is from "Sample Examination Questions" by the NYS Courts: "In this format, each question contains a brief reading selection followed by a question or questions pertaining to the information in the selection. All of the information required to answer the question(s) is provided, so even if the reading selection is on a topic with which you are not familiar, you will be able to answer the question(s) by reading the selection carefully. Remember, answer the questions based only on the information you read in the selection. Do not use any prior knowledge you may have on the subject."[1]

Therefore:
1. Use ONLY the information contained in the passage to answer the questions.
2. Do NOT use prior knowledge to answer the questions.

For example, if you read in a passage that some New York State civil service exams are given in New Jersey (which we know is obviously not true), how would you answer the following question?

1. According to the above passage, which of the following is true?
 A. All New York State civil service exams are given in New York State.
 B. Some New York State civil service exams are given in California.
 C. Some New York State civil service exams are given in New Jersey
 D. No New York State civil service exams are given in New Jersey

In real life, the correct answer is A. HOWEVER, according to the passage, the correct answer is "C" (Some New York State civil service exams are given in New Jersey).

Keep in mind that these questions test for reading skills and NOT prior knowledge. You do not need to have prior knowledge of a subject to answer these questions. All the information needed to answer correctly is in the passage.

However, because some questions may involve information that you are not familiar with, make sure that you take enough time to understand the passage. Read as slowly as necessary and more than once or twice if you need to.

HINT

Read all four choices (A, B, C, and D) and carefully consider each one before deciding which choice is best. Pay careful attention to the details. Match every detail of each choice to the detail in the passage.

The correct answer choice will be the choice that most nearly matches all the details.

(To double-check your answer, make sure that the other choices are not correct because they contain at least one detail that does not match what is stated in the passage.)

Court Officer New York State (NYS Court Officer-Trainee)

Reading comprehension Format A: Sample questions

For the following sample question 1, read the passage and then answer the question based solely on the information provided in the passage.

1. There are twelve ranks of New York State Court Officers. The lowest rank is that of New York State Court Officer-Trainee. To be appointed to this rank, candidates must score well on a written exam and must successfully complete medical, physical, and psychological assessment tests. After two years in the title, Court Officer-Trainees promote to the rank of New York State Court Officer or New York State Senior Court Officer. These three titles have not been assigned an insignia. The lowest title with an insignia is the New York State Court Officer-Sergeant title. This insignia is blue and silver in color. All insignia for titles above New York State Court Officer-Sergeant are gold-colored, with shapes such as a maple leaf, bars and stars. The highest title, Chief of the Department of Public Safety, has an insignia with four gold-colored stars.

According to the above passage, which of the following statements is most accurate?

A. Eight ranks have insignia with gold color.

B. The second highest title has an insignia with two stars.

C. New York State Court Officers promote to New York State Court Officer-Sergeant after two years.

D. One rank has insignia with blue and silver colors and three ranks do not have insignias.

•

1. The correct answer is:
   D. **One rank has insignia with blue and silver color and three ranks do not have insignias**.

"A. Eight ranks have insignia with gold color" is wrong because nine ranks have insignia with gold color.

"B. The second highest title has an insignia with two stars" is wrong because the passage does not state this.

"C. New York State Court Officers promote to New York State Court Officer-Sergeant after two years" is wrong because New York State Court Officer-**Trainees** promote to New York State Court Officer after two years.

•

For the following example question 2, read the passage and then answer the question based solely on the information provided in the passage.

2. Court Officers may be assigned to a variety of duties. One of the most important assignments is providing security in courtrooms, judges' chambers, offices, and public areas. The type of security provided in courtrooms depends on the court. For example, in civil courtrooms, one officer alone may maintain security and assist other personnel and the judge by performing some clerical functions. In criminal courtrooms, Court Officers may transport and secure prisoners during the proceedings. Because of such varied duties, Court Officers must be flexible and ready to "switch gears" as needed. They must have a number of talents and skills, including the ability to apply interpersonal skills. Good judgment and effective communication with many different types of people often prevents negative occurrences and increases the efficiency of court operations.

According to the preceding passage, which of the following statements is most accurate?

A. Court Officers do not need to apply interpersonal skills with criminal defendants.

B. The most important skill of a Court Officer is the ability to use a firearm effectively.

C. New York State Court Officers do not have clerical duties.

D. Court Officers may be assigned to security in public areas.

•

2. The correct answer is: **D. Court Officers may be assigned to security in public areas**. The second sentence states this.

"A. Court officers do not need to apply interpersonal skills with criminal defendants" is wrong because Court Officers always need to apply interpersonal skills.

"B. The most important skill of a Court Officer is the ability to use a firearm effectively" is wrong because this is not mentioned in the passage.

"C. New York State Court Officers do not have clerical duties" is wrong because they perform clerical duties in civil courtrooms.

Reading comprehension Format A: Practice questions

For the following practice questions (1-5) read the passage and then answer the question following the passage based solely on the information provided in the passage.

1. "The Criminal Court of the City of New York is a court of the New York State Unified Court System

in New York City that handles misdemeanors (generally, crimes punishable by fine or imprisonment of up to one year) and lesser offenses, and also conducts arraignments (initial court appearances following arrest) and preliminary hearings in felony cases (generally, more serious offenses punishable by imprisonment of more than one year). It is a single citywide court. The Deputy Chief Administrative Judge for the New York City Courts is responsible for overseeing the day-to-day operations of the NYC trial-level courts, and works with the Administrative Judge of the Criminal Court in order to allocate and assign judicial and nonjudicial personnel resources. One hundred and seven judges may be appointed by the Mayor to 10-year terms, but most of those appointed have been transferred to other courts by the Office of Court Administration."[4]

According to the above passage, which of the following statements is most accurate?

A. Criminal court judges are elected for a term of 10 years.

B. The Chief Administrative Judge is responsible for overseeing the day-to-day operations of the NYC trial-level courts.

C. The maximum term of imprisonment for a misdemeanor is one year.

D. The Criminal Court of the City of New York is a court of the Tri-state Unified Court System.

1. The correct answer is:
   C. **The maximum term of imprisonment for a misdemeanor is one year.**

"**A. Criminal court judges are elected for a term of 10 years**" is wrong because criminal court judges are **appointed** by the mayor.

"**B. The Chief Administrative Judge is responsible for overseeing the day-to-day operations of the NYC trial-level courts**" is wrong because it is the **Deputy** Chief Administrative Judge for the New York City Courts who has that responsibility.

"**D. The Criminal Court of the City of New York is a court of the Tri-state Unified Court System**" is wrong because it is a court of the **New York State** Unified Court System.

•

2. "When a person is called for jury duty in the United States, that service is mandatory and the person summoned for jury duty must attend. Failing to report for jury duty is illegal and usually results in an individual simply being placed back into the selection pool in addition to potential criminal prosecution. Repeatedly ignoring a jury summons without explanation will result in strict penalties, which may include being fined or a bench warrant issued for contempt of court. Employers are not allowed to fire an employee for being called to jury duty, but they are typically not required to pay salaries during this time. When attended, potential jurors may be asked to serve as a juror in a trial, or they may be dismissed.
In the United States, government employees are in a paid status of leave (in accordance with 5 U.S.C. § 6322) for the duration spent serving as a juror (also known as court duty or court leave by some organizations). Many quasi-governmental organizations have adopted this provision into their contract manuals. Accordingly, government employees are in a paid status as long as they have received a summons in connection with a judicial proceeding, by a court or authority responsible for the conduct of that proceeding to serve as a juror (or witness) in the District of Columbia or a state, territory, or possession of the United States, Puerto Rico, or the Trust Territory of the Pacific Islands."[4]

According to the above passage, which of the following choices is not correct?

A. Jury service is mandatory in the United States.

B. A person who fails to report for jury duty is removed from the jury pool.

C. Employers are prohibited from firing an employee for being called to jury duty.

D. Potential jurors may be asked to serve as a juror in a trial, or they may be dismissed.

•

2. The answer is:
"**B. A person who fails to report for jury duty is removed from the jury pool.**" This statement is false because the passage states that "Failing to report for jury duty is illegal and usually results in an individual simply being placed back into the selection pool."

•

3. "Despite the wide variety of uniforms used by United States police departments, virtually all incorporate the use of metallic badges as a means of primary identification. Unlike in the United Kingdom, where officers both in and out of uniform carry - but do not publicly display - paper or plastic

warrant cards, US police badges are the official symbol of office and are prominently worn over the left chest of the uniform (or, in the case of plainclothes officers, displayed from a concealed badge carrier when necessary to establish authority). In Virginia, for instance, police only have the power to make arrests when "in uniform, or displaying a badge of office."

Badges are typically engraved with a unique identification number matched to the officer to whom it is issued. Some departments - most notably the New York City Police Department (NYPD) - traditionally pass individual badges through several generations of police so that current officers can establish a symbolic connection with the retired and deceased officers to whom their badge had previously been issued. In the case of the NYPD, officers who misplace their badge are docked five days of vacation time and many officers wear replica badges to avoid losing their issued badge (though the practice is officially discouraged)."(4)

According to the above passage, which of the following statements is most accurate?

A. All badges of a department have the same identification number.

B. Some badges are used by several generations of officers.

C. Badges must be concealed.

D. Officers who misplace their badge are docked five days of sick leave time.

•

3. The correct answer is: **B. Some badges are used by several generations of officers.**

"A. All badges of a department have the same identification number" is wrong because the passage states that "Badges are typically engraved with a unique identification number."

"C. Badges must be concealed" is wrong because the passage states that "US police badges are the official symbol of office and are prominently worn over the left chest of the uniform."

"D. Officers who misplace their badge are docked five days of sick leave time" is wrong because "officers who misplace their badge are docked five days of **vacation** time."

•

4. "The Miranda warning is part of a preventive criminal procedure rule that law enforcement are required to administer to protect an individual who is in custody and subject to direct questioning or its functional equivalent from a violation of his or her Fifth Amendment right against compelled self-incrimination. In Miranda v. Arizona (1966), the Supreme Court held that the admission of an elicited incriminating statement by a suspect not informed of these rights violates the Fifth Amendment and the Sixth Amendment right to counsel, through the incorporation of these rights into state law. Thus, if law enforcement officials decline to offer a Miranda warning to an individual in their custody, they may interrogate that person and act upon the knowledge gained, but may not use that person's statements as evidence against them in a criminal trial."(4)

According to the above passage, which of the following statements is most accurate?

A. The name Miranda is from a Supreme Court case (1969).

B. Law enforcement officials may decline to offer a Miranda warning to an individual in their custody.

C. The Supreme Court held that the admission of an elicited incriminating statement by a suspect not informed of these rights violates the Seventh Amendment.

D. If law enforcement officials decline to offer a Miranda warning to an individual in their custody, they may interrogate that person and act upon the knowledge gained, and may use that person's statements as evidence against them in a criminal trial.

•

The correct answer is:
"B. <u>Law enforcement officials may decline to offer a Miranda warning to an individual in their custody</u>."

"A. The name Miranda is from a Supreme Court case (1969)" is wrong because the correct year is <u>**1966**</u>.

"C. The Supreme Court held that the admission of an elicited incriminating statement by a suspect not informed of these rights violates the Seventh Amendment" is wrong because it violates the <u>**Fifth**</u> and <u>**Sixth**</u> Amendments.

"D. If law enforcement officials decline to offer a Miranda warning to an individual in their custody, they may interrogate that person and act upon the knowledge gained, and may use that person's statements as evidence against them in a criminal trial" is wrong because they may <u>**not**</u> use the person's statements against him in a criminal trial.

•

5. **CPL 2.10 Persons designated as peace officers**
Notwithstanding the provisions of any general, special or local law or charter to the contrary, only the following persons shall have the powers of, and shall be peace officers:
1. Constables or police constables of a town or village, provided such designation is not inconsistent with local law.
2. The sheriff, undersheriff and deputy sheriffs of New York city and sworn officers of the Westchester county department of public safety services appointed after January thirty-first, nineteen hundred eighty-three to the title of public safety officer and who perform the functions previously performed by
a Westchester county deputy sheriff on or prior to such date.
3. Investigators of the office of the state commission of investigation.

•

5. According to the above passage, which of the following statements is most accurate?

A. The persons listed in this article shall have the power of and be police officers.

B. Sworn officers of the Westchester county department of public safety services appointed after 1/31/1993 are designated as peace officers.

C. The undersheriff of New York city is a peace officer.

D. All three statements (A, B, and C) are correct.

•

The correct answer is **"C. The undersheriff of New York city is a peace officer."**

"A. The persons listed in this article shall have the power of and be police officers" is wrong because the passage deals with peace officers and **not** police officers.

"B. Sworn officers of the Westchester county department of public safety services appointed after 1/31/1993 are designated as peace officers" is wrong because "Sworn officers of the Westchester county department of public safety services appointed after **January thirty-first, nineteen hundred eighty-three** are designated as peace officers.

"D. All three statements (A, B, and C) are correct" is not the best answer because statements A and B are wrong.

Format B (Missing Words): Select the best alternative from four alternatives that best completes a sentence or passage.

This type of question tests your ability to understand the logic of a sentence and your familiarity with basic spelling, vocabulary, and grammar. These abilities are important when you need to construct sentences that are clear and that convey your intended meaning.

The following is from "Sample Examination Questions" by the NYS Courts: "In this format the test contains a short, written passage from which some words have been omitted. You need to select one word from the four alternatives that best completes the passage."

Here is an example of this type of question:

Example 1: In the following passage, five words have been omitted. For each omitted word, select one word from the four alternatives that best completes the passage.

Court Officers assigned to magnetometer posts must be ____1____ to prevent unauthorized weapons from being brought into court buildings. ____2____ generally known that a significant number of persons carry ____3____ weapons. In carrying out their security duties, Court Officers must strive to be ____4____ to avoid an unnecessary distraction from the efficient processing of other court visitors. The flow of visitors must be smooth to avoid clogging the ____5____ between the magnetometers.

1. a. vigilent	2. a. Its	3. a. congealed	4. a. discrete	5. a. ailles
b. vigillent	b. Its'	b. concerted	b. discreet	b. ails
c. vigilant	c. It	c. concealed	c. diskreet	c. isles
d. vigelent	d. It's	d. cancelled	d. discerned	d. aisles

•

Answers 1 - 5

1. **C** (Correct spelling)
2. **D** ("It's" is the contraction for "It is.")
3. **C** ("Concealed" means "hidden.")
4. **B** ("Discreet" means to "not draw attention.")
5. **D** ("Aisles" means "the passage between rows.")

Example 2: In the following passage, five words have been omitted. For each omitted word, select one word from the four alternatives that best completes the passage.

Proper courtroom decorum is vital for court efficiency and appreciation of the importance of court proceedings. Maintaining good behavior and propriety is not an easy task. For example, in almost every courtroom there is a notice _____1_____ the use of cell phones during court proceedings. However, some members of the public routinely disregard the notices. The biggest two offenders of this rule _____2_____ teenage boys and girls. The reason is not that they wish to be _____3_____; usually it's because they have developed a "cell phone" habit they can't seem to break. When cell phone are confiscated, they are placed in an _____4_____ and usually returned at the _____5_____ of the court session.

1. a. approving	2. a. is	3. a. agreeable	4. a. envelop	5. a. start
b. prohibiting	b. becomes	b. abiding	b. envellope	b. close
c. aiding	c. breaches	c. disrespectful	c. ennvelope	c. height
d. allowing	d. are	d. helpful	d. envelope	d. zenith

•

Answers 1 - 5

1. **B** (prohibiting, for the logic of the sentence)
2. **D** (are, because it refers to plural boys and girls)
3. **C** (disrespectful, for the logic of the sentence.)
4. **D** (envelope, for the spelling)
5. **B** (close, for the logic of the sentence.)

HINT!

Even if you are certain of the answer, read that section with that word (and also each of the other choices) to make sure that the word you selected is the best choice. Also, try to make it clear in your mind why each of the rejected choices is not a better choice.

Practice Exercises

Directions: This section contains 5 passages. In each passage five words or phrases have been omitted. For each omitted word, select the one word or phrase from the four alternatives that best completes the passage.

Passage 1:

Court Officers may be assigned to a building-wide security detail. Because of this, _____1_____ necessary for them to have on hand a variety of equipment. Three of these equipment tools _____2_____ handcuffs, flashlight, and a radio. All three of these _____3_____ building search and securing of suspects. Of course, there are other tools, which are _____4_____. Without these items, _____5_____ Court Officer may sustain serious injury.

1. a. its	2. a. is	3. a. facilitates	4. a. superfluous	5. a. many
b. is	b. aren't	b. facillitate	b. neccessary	b. some
c. it's	c. are;	c. facilitate	c. supperflous	c. a
d. it	d. are:	d. faciletate	d. necessary	d. all

Answers 1 - 5

1. **C** it's ("It's" means "it is".)
2. **D** are (A colon is used to direct attention to a list.)
3. **C** facilitate (correct spelling and plural)
4. **D** necessary (correct spelling and logical meaning)
5. **C** a (refers to one Court Officer)

Passage 2:

In a civil jury trial there is a jury comprised of six regular jurors and usually two alternates. Their duty is to render an _____6_____ verdict. Because of this, all members of the _____7_____ must listen _____8_____ to the witnesses and must apply the law that the judge communicates to them. The verdict rendered by them may be unanimous or must comprise the agreement of 5 out of the _____9_____ regular jurors. The alternate jurors _____10_____ usually dismissed when the regular jury retires to deliberate. However, the judge may order that they remain in a waiting room in case one of the regular jurors becomes ill and cannot continue with the deliberations.

6. a. partial	7. a. team	8. a. recklessly	9. a. eight	10.a. were
b. impartial	b. squad	b. forgetfully	b. six	b. is
c. prejudicial	c. jury	c. rashly	c. five	c. are
d. prenuptial	d. crowd	d. carefully	d. seven	d. isn't

Answers 6 - 10

6. **B** impartial (vocabulary; "Impartial" means "fair and just".)
7. **C** jury (logic and consistency)
8. **D** carefully (vocabulary and logic)
9. **B** six (logic)
10. **C** are (tense, grammar and logic)

Passage 3:

The Court Officer-Trainee Exam is not an easy exam. The reason for this fact _____11_____ the many abilities that it tests. The main abilities tested by this exam _____12_____ good judgment and reading skills. To _____13_____ success on the test, we recommend that you develop your reading skills and answer "judgment questions" based on commonly agreed upon management _____14_____. Also, care should be taken not to answer questions in a way that _____15_____ disregard for stated court rules and objectives.

11. a. are	12. a. is	13. a. ensur	14. a. principals	15. a. hides
b. were	b. are	b. insur	b. princepels	b. displays
c. aren't	c. were	c. insuer	c. principles	c. obscures
d. is	d. aren't	d. ensure	d. princeples	d. omits

Answers 11 - 15

11. **D** is (The subject is singular "reason"; therefore singular verb used is "is" instead of "are.")
12. **B** are ("Are" is plural and agrees with the plural subject "main abilities.")
13. **D** ensure (spelling, "Ensure" means "to guarantee" that something will happen.)
14. **C** principles ("Principles" means "basic rules or beliefs.")
15. **B** displays (logic)

Passage 4:

On Monday morning, a tip was received by Court Officers headquarters that an individual on the NYC Warrants List would be appearing as a witness in Part 15 on an unrelated case. His wanted file indicated that he had a skull and bone _____16_____ on his left shoulder. The file also indicated that he was a _____17_____ violent offender and that he had already been found guilty on three felonies committed at different times. One felony conviction was for _____18_____ of drugs. At approximately 11:00 a.m., he was located and detained by Court Officer William Jenkins. Upon his arrest, he stated that he had not _____19_____ any crimes and that he had always been framed. Court Officer Jenkins recited the Miranda Rights and told him that it was not _____20_____ that he speak without first consulting with an attorney.

16. a.tattu	17. a. persistant	18. a. rebuttal	19. a. comitted	20. a. illogical
b. tatoo	b. persestent	b. permitting	b. committed	b. advisable
c. tatu	c. persistent	c. positioning	c. commited	c. adviseable
d. tattoo	d. persestint	d. possession	d. comited	d. advizable

Answers 16 - 20

16. **D** tattoo (correct spelling)
17. **C** persistent (correct spelling)
18. **D** possession (correct spelling, meaning and logic)
19. **B** committed (correct spelling)
20. **B** advisable (logic and meaning)

•

Passage 5:

Court Officer Juanita Williamson was patrolling the fourth floor when she saw a teenager spitting on the hallway floor. She _____21_____ the teenager and informed him that there was a rest room on the fourth floor. The teenager acted in a _____22_____ manner by spitting on the floor again. When Court Officer Williamson asked him for his name, he answered in an _____23_____ manner. Because she could not understand anything he said, she suspected that the teenager was acting under the _____24_____ of alcohol. However, before Court Officer Williamson could take any action, the teenager fainted and fell to the floor. She noticed that his complexion was _____25_____ and his breathing was labored. She summoned the Court Officer medic team who quickly transported him to the medical office.

21.a. estolled	22. a. graceful	23. a. cogent	24. a. affluence	25. a. strong
b. praised	b. belligerent	b. precise	b. influence	b. hardy
c. admonished	c. pacific	c. clear	c. infusion	c. healthy
d. lauded	d. peaceful	d. incoherent	d. affability	d. pallid

•

Answers 21 - 25

21. **C** admonished (vocabulary; "Admonished" means "reprimanded".)
22. **B** belligerent (logic, "Belligerent" means "combative".)
23. **D** incoherent ("incoherent" means "expressed in a confusing way")
24. **B** influence (correct spelling, vocabulary, and usage)
25. **D** pallid (logic; "Pallid" means "pale because of poor health".)

CHAPTER 5: Applying Facts and Information to Given Situations

"This section of the written exam assesses your ability to take information which you have read and apply it to a specific situation defined by a given set of facts.

Each question contains a brief passage which describes a regulation, procedure or law. The selection is followed by a description of a specific situation. Then a question is asked which requires you to apply the law, regulation, or procedure described in the passage to the specific situation.

Remember that all of the information you need to answer the question is contained in the passage and in the description of the situation. You need to read and understand both before you attempt to answer the question."[1]

•

Procedure Situation Questions
(Law, Regulation, or Procedure)

Example 1: The following question contains a Rule and a Situation. Read both, then answer the question by applying the Rule.

Rule: In a civil trial, persons who are scheduled to appear as witnesses or who may be called as witnesses shall not remain in the courtroom during any part of the trial before they are called to testify. They must wait in a place outside the courtroom until they are called into the courtroom to appear as witnesses. This applies to persons who are minors or adults. In all cases, the presiding judge shall inform the public in the courtroom of this rule and shall not start or continue with the trial until such notice has been given. Any objections or disputes or uncertainty among attorneys or court personnel regarding the allowable presence of persons in the courtroom shall be referred to the presiding judge who shall make a determination.

Situation: Court Officer Albert Holmes is assigned to Part 10, a civil court trial courtroom where Judge Nora Appleton is presiding. Before the trial starts, Jack Abrams, a person sitting in the courtroom, mentions to Officer Holmes that he is there to appear as a witness.

1. Based on the above rule and situation, which of the following is the best action that Court Officer Holmes should take?

A. Inform Mr. Abrams that he is disqualified to be a witness because he was sitting in the courtroom.
B. Inform Mr. Abrams that he may sit in the courtroom because he is a member of the public.
C. Inform Mr. Abrams that he may wait with the jury in the jury room.
D. Inform Judge Appleton that a prospective witness is present in the courtroom.

Answer: **D. Inform Judge Appleton that a prospective witness is present in the courtroom.**

Choice A is wrong because such a disqualification determination should be made by the judge and not by a court officer.

Choice B is wrong because prospective witnesses may not sit in the courtroom.

Choice C is wrong because having a witness sit with the jury who will decide the case is illogical and prejudicial.

Example 2: The following question contains a rule (section of law) and a situation. Read both, then answer the question by applying the law.

Rule: Family Court Act, Section 812: For purposes of this article, "members of the same family or household" shall mean the following:

    (a) persons related by consanguinity or affinity;

    (b) persons legally married to one another;

    (c) persons formerly married to one another regardless of whether they still reside in the same household;

    (d) persons who have a child in common regardless of whether such persons have been married or have lived together at any time...."

A petition filed against a person listed in this section shall be known as an "FCA 812 Petition." The clerk shall accept all filings, with a determination as to the further processing of such filings to be made by the Judge Presiding in Part 20.

Situation: A member of the public, Brenda Wagner, approaches Court Officer Harriet Egger and states that she wishes to file a Family Court Family Offense petition ("FCA 812 Petition") against her friend, Cynthia Farmer, for verbal abuse. She remarks that a year earlier she had successfully filed an FCA 812 Petition against her husband.

2. Based on the preceding Rule and Situation, which of the following four choices is the best course of action for Court Officer Harriet Egger to follow?

A. Inform Ms. Wagner that she should file a case and also sue for money damages.

B. Direct Ms. Wagner to the Family Offense Intake and Information counter where they can process her request.

C. Inform Ms. Wagner that she is in the wrong court.

D. Inform Ms. Wagner that based on the facts, she does not qualify under section 812 and that trying to file a case under section 812 would be a waste of time.

Answer: <u>B. Direct Ms. Wagner to the Family Offense Intake and Information counter where they can process her request.</u>

Choice A is wrong because the determination as to whether her case should be filed should be made by the Judge in Part 20. Also, Court Officers should not influence litigants on whether or not to sue.

Choice C is wrong because the decision on the proper court should be made by the Judge in Part 20.

Choice D is wrong because Court Officers should not act as gatekeepers for access to the court, as section 812 specifically states that the clerk shall accept all filings.

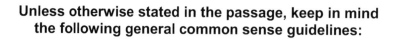

**Unless otherwise stated in the passage, keep in mind
the following general common sense guidelines:**

Court Officers on duty must be in proper uniform and act professionally.

Court officers must not give legal advice or advice on how to proceed on a case.

Court officers should refer people to the right office or courtroom and not act as gatekeepers by making determinations.

Court officers should not make decisions outside their scope of employment.

Court officers should not guess when they are not sure on how to respond to an inquiry.

Court Officers must maintain the appearance of being impartial and not take sides in legal disputes.

When necessary and possible, Court Officers should ask for support from additional Court Officers support instead of taking unnecessary risks.

Court officers assigned to courtrooms work in tandem with clerical supervisors in the courtroom and the judge presiding in the courtroom.

Directions: The following section contains 10 questions. Each question contains a brief passage which describes a law, regulation or procedure. The selection is followed by a description of a specific situation. Then a question is asked which requires you to apply the law, regulation, or procedure described in the passage to the specific situation.

Question 1:

Regulation:
The following are general guidelines which Court Officers follow when carrying out their duties. As with all guidelines, deviation from the guidelines may sometimes be necessary. However, the deviation should be logical and in the best interests of the public and the court.
1. Court Officers on duty must be in proper uniform and act in a professional manner.
2. Court Officers must not give legal advice or advice on how to proceed on a case.
3. Court Officers should refer people to the right office or courtroom and not act as gatekeepers by making determinations.
4. Court Officers should not make decisions outside their scope of employment.
5. Court Officers should not guess when they are not sure on how to respond to an inquiry.
6. Court Officers must maintain the appearance of being impartial and not take sides in legal disputes.
7. When necessary and possible, Court Officers should ask for additional Court Officers support and not take unnecessary risks.

Situation:
Before the start of her tour, and before she has had time to change out of her civilian clothes and into her uniform, Court Officer Juliet Huang witnesses a mother and daughter arguing in the criminal court hallway. The daughter is insisting on filing a family offense proceeding in the criminal court where they now are. However, the mother is saying that it would be more prudent to start the case in family court. The arguing is intense and loud and Court Officer Huang understands that she must stop the argument before it disrupts the proceedings in the nearby courtrooms.

1. According to the above procedure and situation, what is the best action for Court Officer Juliet Huang to take?

A. Do nothing and let someone else eventually handle it because she is out of uniform.
B. Explain to the mother and daughter that she understands the concurrent jurisdiction of family court and criminal court regarding family offense proceedings and because of that, the case must be filed in family court.
C. Identify herself as a Court Officer and speak with the mother and daughter and ask them to go into a nearby waiting room where they may continue their discussion, or go to the clerk's office where they may ask their questions regarding initiating a proceeding.
D. Inform them not to start the case because they are both visibly argumentative and they would in all probability lose the case.

•

Question 2:

Procedure:
One of the duties of Court Officers assigned to magnetometer stations is to determine if any court visitor is carrying a weapon, either authorized or unauthorized. If a weapon is not authorized, the weapon must be confiscated, and an unusual incident report must be filed by the Court Officer before the close of business. If the weapon is authorized, the Court Officer must secure the weapon in the security safe and must issue a receipt to the owner of the weapon, who may at any time after he has finished his court business and before the end of the court day produce the receipt and retrieve his weapon. If possession of the unauthorized weapon is contrary to NYS law, the Court Officer Major must be consulted, and action taken as per the Major's order, made after a review by the Major.

Court Officer New York State (NYS Court Officer-Trainee)

Situation:
Court Officer Shela Jenkins is working at a magnetometer station when she spots a knife in the pocket of a male visitor. She obtains the knife and asks the visitor to wait on the side while she decides what to do.

2. According to the above procedure and situation, what is the best action for Court Officer Shela Jenkins to take?

A. She should handcuff the person and arrest him for possessing a knife.
B She should return the knife to the person if he agrees to keep it concealed while at court.
C. She should ask the person where he obtained the knife.
D. She should secure the knife and speak with her supervisor regarding further action.

•

Question 3:

Regulation:
"NYS Court Officer-Trainees are peace officers, required to wear uniforms, and may be authorized to carry firearms, execute bench warrants and make arrests. Typical duties include: guarding and escorting criminal defendants while in the court facility; escorting judges, juries and witnesses; handling court documents and forms; providing information and assistance to the public and other court users; maintaining the security of deliberating and sequestered juries; displaying and safeguarding exhibits; operating security equipment and using established search procedures; physically restraining and calming unruly individuals; administering first-aid and assistance to individuals during emergencies; and performing related duties."(2)

Situation:
Court Officer James Chin is assigned to a criminal courtroom where he is responsible for guarding criminal defendant Benjamin Lambert. During a 20 minute court recess, Benjamin Lambert informs Court Officer Chin that he needs to use the restroom. The sequestered jury is using the only available restroom in the building. Another restroom is available across the street, in the criminal court annex building. Court Officer Lambert must decide how to deal with Mr. Lambert's request.

3. Based on the above regulation and situation, which of the following four choices is the best course of action for Court Officer Chin to take?

A. Court Officer Chin should tell Mr. Lambert that he should have used the restroom before the start of proceedings.
B. Court Officer Chin should knock on the restroom door and ask the jurors to hurry because the defendant needs to use the restroom.
C. Court Officer Chin should inform the judge, and with the judge's permission and additional court officer support, he should escort Mr. Lambert to an available restroom in the criminal court annex across the street.
D. Court Officer Chin should not take any action.

Question 4:

Regulation:
The ADA (American With Disabilities Act) requires that public facilities provide reasonable accommodations for persons with disabilities. Because of this, courtrooms must have a space available where a person in a wheelchair may be situated during court proceedings. The Part 12 courtroom, where Court Officer Juanita Rodriguez is assigned, has a space in the audience area designated for this purpose.

Situation:
At 10:05 a.m., after the start of the court session on Monday morning, a person in a wheelchair enters the courtroom. Because it is a Monday, the courtroom is very crowded, with some people standing in the back of the courtroom. Attorney Fred Williker is standing in the spot where a wheelchair is usually situated. Court Officer Rodriguez asks Mr. Williker to please move to the side so that the person in the wheelchair can have the spot. Mr. Williker refuses to move and informs Court Officer Rodriguez that he is there to answer the calendar call and that there is no other spot where he can move to.

4. Based on the above regulation and situation, which of the following four choices is the best course of action for Court Officer Rodriguez to take?

A. Make an announcement that court cannot proceed until this matter is resolved.
B. Discreetly speak with the judge to obtain his input as to Mr. Williker's concern regarding his need to be present for the calendar call.
C. Inform Mr. Williker that he will be arrested if he does not move out of the way.
D. Inform the person in the wheelchair that there is no available space and that he must leave the courtroom.

Question 5:

Regulation:
"Incident Reports" are required to be completed and filed for situations that need to be reported to Court Officer Headquarters. "General Incident Report, Form IR-701" is used to report any unusual occurrence that does not involve any medical intervention. An "Assisted Incident Report, Form IR-107" is used when first aid is administered, or an ambulance is summoned, or any other type of medical assistance is provided. Both reports must be completed as soon as possible and must be filed before the close of the court day.

Situation:
During her roaming security detail, Court Officer Janet Damico notices two individuals who are taking the down elevator and are exchanging money and what appears to be a pouch of white powder. She reports what she saw by radio and minutes later learns that the two individuals have been arrested on the first floor for possession of drugs. Court Officer Damico is required to file an incident report. However, it is close to 5:00 pm. She is tired and would rather file the report next morning when she is refreshed and more alert.

5. Based on the above regulation and situation, which of the following four choices is the best course of action for Court Officer Damico to take?

A. Since Court Officer Damico did not make the arrest, she does not have to file an incident report.
B. Even though she is tired, she must try to complete and file Form RI-107 before the end of the court day.
C. She should radio headquarters and inform them that she will file Form IR-107 the following morning.

D. She must file Form IR-701 before the close of the court day, and inform headquarters if there is any reason that she cannot file it in time.

Question 6:

Procedure:
A NYS Court Officer who is the recipient of a bomb threat must do the following in the sequence specified:
1. First, stay calm and do not hang up.
2. In a calm voice, engage the caller in a conversation. If possible, write down exactly what the caller is saying.
3. Signal, or write a message to a fellow officer or other employee of the court and write down the number of the caller, if displayed on your phone.
4. Do not hang up your phone, even after the caller hangs up. The reason for this is that the call may sometimes be traced if the line remains open.
5. Use another phone to report the call to the "Bomb Threat Headquarters."

Situation:
Court Officer Nora Bartek is assigned to answer telephones in the Court Officers Headquarters during the lunch hour. During that time, she receives a call from a male who states that he has placed a bomb in the court building and then quickly hangs up.

6. Based on the procedure and situation, which of the following four choices is the best course of action for Court Officer Bartek to take?

A. Hang up the phone and immediately call "Bomb Threat Headquarters."
B. Immediately contact the main offices in the building and inform them of the bomb threat.
C. Do not hang up the phone and use a different phone to contact "Bomb Threat Headquarters."
D. Try to contact the Court Officer Major in the building.

Question 7:

Regulation: Small Claims actions may be initiated by filling out the required forms at the Small Claims Office and paying the required filing and postage fees. The basic fee for each action (where there is one defendant) is $20.00 plus $4.75 postage fee. If an action has more than one defendant, an additional postage fee of $4.75 is charged for each additional defendant.

Situation: A member of the public, Samuel Livona, wishes to file two Small Claims actions. The first action is against two defendants and the second action is against three defendants. He asks Court Officer Mark Udall what the total fee for the two cases is.

7. Based on the above regulation and situation, which of the following four choices is the correct total amount that Samuel Livona must pay for the two cases?

A. $ 49.50
B. $ 54.25
C. $ 59.00
D. $ 63.75

Question 8:

Procedure: Court Officers who are assigned to security, both courtroom and facilities security, should be vigilant in spotting any ongoing situation that may be of concern or might develop into a problematic situation. Depending on the situation and time available, it is vital that Court Officers contact in a timely manner the appropriate emergency teams and Court Officer Headquarters. However, routine and non-emergency matters that are usually handled by individual Court Officers should continue to be so handled without unnecessarily drawing on additional security or emergency resources.

Situation:
Court Officer Antonio Fitzgerald is assigned to hallway security. While on the sixth floor, he notices that a locked electrical panel has been pried open and that large sparks are violently coming out of it. He looks around and estimates that there are at least twenty people near the panel.

8. Based on the above procedure, which of the following four choices is the best first action for Court Officer Fitzgerald to take?

A. Take immediate action by questioning everyone present to determine if any of them have any information on who pried open the panel.
B. Examine the electrical panel for at least a few minutes to see if there is any chance of it starting a fire in the building.
C. Immediately have all the members of the public step away from the electrical panel.
D. Call Court Officer Headquarters and report the situation with the electrical panel.

•

Question 9:

Regulation:
Court Officers must use proper judgment when responding to situations, including situations that involve injury to persons or property. Prioritization of available responses should be based on the descending order of severity and need to act quickly. Because of this, Court Officers must be able to apply mature and sound judgment to a variety of situations. Rigid and absolute rules are therefore seldom found in the Court Officer Manual. Instead, guidelines and suggested responses are provided, thereby giving Court Officers the necessary leeway to decide on the best solution.

Situation:
While patrolling the hallway leading to the basement parking area, Officer Edward Douglas hears a crashing noise, including the sound of glass breaking. He rushes down the hall and sees a middle-aged male on the floor, next to a large metal and glass fire emergency equipment case that had been mounted on the wall. The man's arm is bleeding profusely and the man is pleading for help.

9. Based on the above procedure, which of the following four choices is the best first action for Court Officer Douglas to take?

A. For reasons of assignment of liability and incident reporting, ask the man if he had been tampering with the metal case before it fell.
B. Quickly get the name and address of the person in case the loss of blood renders him unconscious.
C. Ask the man which of his relatives he wishes to be contacted regarding the incident.
D. Apply first aid procedures to stop the loss of blood and then contact Court Officers Headquarters for assistance.

Question 10:

Procedure:
Court Officers are required to be in uniform and at their post at the start of their shift. Because of this, Court Officers receive 15 minutes of extra daily compensation, for time needed to dress appropriately. Court Officers who arrive at their post late, after the start of their shift, may receive an informal counseling memo from their Sergeant for each infraction. After three infractions within any 180-day period, they may be formally counseled by their Major and may be subject to disciplinary action such as reduction of pay for each infraction during the prior 180-day period.

Situation:
Court Officer Ronald Baker arrived late to his assigned post on January 7, March 26, and July 22.

10. Based on the procedure and situation, Court Officer Baker's sergeant may:

A. Issue Court Officer Baker another informal counseling memo because he has accumulated three memos in a 180-day period.
B. Formally counsel Court Officer Baker.
C. Order a reduction in pay for Court Officer Baker.
D. Remind Court Officer Baker that after three infractions within any 180-day period, he may be formally counseled and subject to other disciplinary action.

•

Answers for preceding 10 questions:

1. C. Identify herself as a Court Officer and speak with the mother and daughter and ask them to go into a nearby waiting room where they may continue their discussion, or go to the clerk's office where they may ask their questions regarding initiating a proceeding.
Choice A is wrong because even though the Court Officer is not in uniform that should not prevent her from trying to resolve a dispute that would interfere with court proceedings.
Choice B is wrong because whether or not Court Officer Huang is knowledgeable in criminal law, she should not act as a gatekeeper nor give legal advice.
Choice D is wrong because Court Officer Huang must be impartial and not act as a gatekeeper or give illogical advice.

2. D. She should secure the knife and speak with her supervisor regarding further action.
The knife might be within legal limits. However, it probably should not be brought into court. For this reason, she should not act prematurely or arrest the person, but should at minimum consult with her supervisor as to what the next step should be.

3. C. Court Officer Chin should inform the judge, and with the judge's permission and additional Court Officer support, he should escort Mr. Lambert to an available restroom in the criminal court annex across the street.
(Choice A, rebuking the defendant, is illogical and counterproductive, just as is choice B. Choice D (not doing anything) would complicate court proceedings once they are resumed. Therefore, choice C is the best choice. The Court Officer informs the judge, gets permission, and proceeds, with additional security.)

4. B. Discreetly speak with the judge to obtain his input as to Mr. Williker's concern regarding his need to be present for the calendar call.
Choice A is not necessary and an overreach of authority by the Court Officer.
Choices C and D are harsh and unnecessary solutions. The needs of all persons should be considered, if possible, in a non-confrontational manner.

5. D. She must file Form IR-701 before the close of the court day, and inform headquarters if there is any reason that she cannot file it in time.
Choice a is not correct because she was involved in the incident and is required to file a report.
Choices B and C refer to "Form IR-107" which reports medical assistance and is not the correct form for this situation.

6. C. Do not hang up the phone and use a different phone to contact "Bomb Threat Headquarters."
Choice A is wrong because the procedure specifically states not to hang up the phone.
Choice B is wrong because the procedure does not mention that course of action. Also, doing this might cause major concern in the building.
Choice D is wrong because the procedure requires notifying the "Bomb Threat Headquarters" and does not mention notifying the Major.

7. D. $ 63.75
Case #1: $20.00 + $4.75 = $24.75 (for the first defendant)
$\underline{ + \$ \ 4.75}$ (for the second defendant
Total $29.50 for the first case.

Case #2: $20.00 + $4.75 = $24.75 (for the first defendant)
$\underline{ + \$ \ 9.50}$ ($4.75 for second defendant + $4.75 for third defendant)
Total $34.25 for the second case.

Case #1: $29.50 + Case #2: $34.25 = **Total of $63.75 for both cases**.

8. C. Immediately have all the members of the public step away from the electrical panel.
Because of the very dangerous situation, Court Officer Fitzgerald must take immediate action. Priority is making sure that nearby people are not injured. This can be achieved with a few quick verbal commands to step away, and then he should contact Headquarters.

9. D. Apply first aid procedures to stop the loss of blood and then contact Court Officers Headquarters for assistance.
This is the best first action for Court Officer Douglas to take. A timely response of stopping the loss of blood will prevent the man from bleeding to death and will provide time to call for assistance.

10. D. Remind Court Officer Baker that after three infractions within any 180-day period, he may be formally counseled and subject to other disciplinary action.
(All the other answer choices (A, B, and C) are not authorized by the procedure, especially since Officer Baker only had two informal counseling memos during the preceding 180-day period.

Answer key

1. C	6. C
2. D	7. D
3. C	8. C
4. B	9. D
5. D	10. D

CHAPTER 6: Remembering Facts and Information

Remembering Facts and Information Questions have been on every Court Officer exam since the early 1980s. A reason for this is that Court Officers need to remember many details to do their work properly. Among other facts, they need to keep in mind the many rules and regulations that affect their peace officer duties, information needed to respond to inquiries from the public, and also the locations of courtrooms and offices in large court buildings, the types and frequency of cases that are handled, and the names of other Court Officers and court personnel, including Judges and Supervisors.

How this portion of the test is administered: (Usually this is the first part of the test.)

"You will be provided with a written description of an incident (story) on a one page form and given five (5) minutes to read and study the story.
At the end of the 5-minute period, the story will be removed and you will not have another opportunity to refer back to it.
You will not be permitted to make any written notes about the story.
There will be a 10-minute delay before you receive your test question booklet.
You will then be asked a series of questions about the facts concerning the story." [1]

Other details:
The passage is usually under one page long (approximately 300-400 words).
A typical candidate can read the passage carefully 2-3 times within the allotted 5 minutes.
The number of questions that are asked is usually about 10 to 15.

HINTS

1. Use a watch to keep track of the time. (Only" traditional" or "simple digital" watches are usually permitted.)

2. Use ALL the time that you are allowed.

3. Read the passage the first time to get a general overview of the content. Try to remember major facts and details.

4. Read the passage once again. This time try to remember smaller details.

5. Try to connect or arrange the details (order the details) in a way that will help you remember them. (For example: numbers in ascending or descending order, names or titles in alphabetical order, locations (example rooms) by building or other geographical order.) If creating a "mental picture" of the connected details is helpful, then do so.

6. Make sure that you keep in memory the details regarding "Who? What? When? and Where? of the passage.

7. Make sure that you answer ALL the questions.

8. If there is a question that you don't know the answer to, give it your best guess. In past Court Officers exams, candidates were not penalized for answering wrong (unlike some exams where points are deducted for each question answered incorrectly.)

Court Officer New York State (NYS Court Officer-Trainee)

Example of directions:

When instructed by the test monitor, turn this page over and for the next 5 minutes read the passage on the page as many times as you want. Try to memorize as many details of the passage as you can. At the end of the 5 minutes, when the test monitor instructs you to do so, stop reading and turn the page over. The test monitor will then collect this page.

(After the next 10 minutes, the test monitor will distribute the test booklets. When instructed to do so by the test monitor, open the test booklet and answer the first 10 questions in the booklet.)

Example of a Passage:

On October 5, 2018, Janet Brighton began her first day of jury service. As directed by the jury notice, she reported at 9:30 a.m. to the civil court central jury room on the second floor of 165 Schermerhorn Street, Brooklyn, New York, 11202. The room was supervised by three court clerks, two females and one male. The male clerk, named Peter Jamieson, called a list of twenty-five juror names. Janet's name was one of the names called.

About fifteen minutes after the names were called, a female Court Officer named Wilma Madison arrived and announced that they would be going up to the ninth floor courtroom, Part 21C (presided over by Judge Mark Unger), where they would be questioned by attorneys for possible juror service on a motor vehicle accident case that involved personal injury and property damages. Because they could not all fit in one elevator, they were divided into two groups. Another Court Officer, Thomas Dellano, arrived and escorted one group while Court Officer Wilma Madison escorted the second group.

In the courtroom, the first eight jurors who had been called by Clerk Peter Jamieson were seated in the jury box while the remaining jurors took seats in the public benches of the courtroom. Two attorneys took turns questioning the first eight prospective jurors. The names of the attorneys were Brenda Faulkner, who represented the plaintiff, and Margaret Numbria, who represented the defendant. The attorneys questioned the eight jurors and thereafter questioned another ten jurors. By the time they decided on the final eight jurors (six for the regular jury and two for the alternates) a total of ten jurors had been dismissed. The remaining seven jurors were not questioned and were also dismissed.

After jury selection was completed and before the case was adjourned, the Judge thanked all the jurors present, directed them not to discuss the case with anyone, and to return the following morning.

> Remember that usually, at the end of 5 minutes, the test monitor will instruct you to stop reading. At that time please stop reading and turn this page over. The test monitor will then collect this page.
>
> (After the next 10 minutes, the test monitor will distribute the test booklets. When instructed to do so by the test monitor, open the test booklet and answer the first 10 questions in the booklet.)

Questions 1-10

1. The date that Ms. Brighton began her first day of jury service was:
   A. October 2, 2018
   B. October 9, 2018
   C. October 5, 2018
   D. October 4, 2018

2. Ms. Brighton's first name is:
   A. Wilma
   B. Margaret
   C. Janet
   D. None of the above

3. The courtroom where the jurors were taken for questioning was on the _____ floor.
   A. second
   B. ninth
   C. sixth
   D. fifth

4. The last name of the Court Officer whose first name was Thomas and that that took some jurors up to the courtroom was:
   A. Dellano
   B. Madison
   C. Jamieson
   D. Brighton

5. The civil court central jury room had three clerks assigned. They were:
   A. 3 females
   B. 2 females and 1 male
   C. 3 males
   D. 2 males and 1 female

6. The number of the Part where the jurors were taken is:
   A. Part 12D
   B. Part 21C
   C. Part 21D
   D. Part 12C

7. How many jurors were on the regular jury?
   A. 6
   B. 8
   C. 18
   D. 25

8. The name of the attorney that represented the plaintiff was:
   A. Brenda Faulkner
   B. James Brighton
   C. Thomas Dellano
   D. Margaret Numbria

9. At what time did the subject of this passage report for jury duty?
   A. 9:00 a.m.
   B. 9:15 a.m.
   C. 9:30 a.m.
   D. 10:00 a.m.

10. How many prospective jurors were not questioned and dismissed?
   A. 10
   B. 8
   C. 18
   D. 7

•

Answers 1-10

1. C. October 5, 2018

2. C. Janet

3. B. ninth

4. A. Dellano

5. B. 2 females and 1 male

6. B. Part 21C

7. A. 6

8. A. Brenda Faulkner

9. C. 9:30 a.m.

10. D. 7

For practice, do the following three memory questions.

Court Officer New York State (NYS Court Officer-Trainee)

Memory Passage 1:

Directions:

When instructed by the test monitor, turn this page over and for the next 5 minutes read the passage on the page as many times as you want. Try to memorize as many details of the passage as you can. At the end of the 5 minutes, when the test monitor instructs you to do so, stop reading and turn the page over. The test monitor will then collect this page.

(After the next 10 minutes, the test monitor will distribute the test booklets. When instructed to do so by the test monitor, open the test booklet and answer the first 10 questions in the booklet.)

Three Court Officer-Trainees who graduated from the Court Officer Academy together and who had become friends at the Academy, were assigned to three different courts in New York City. All three were very happy with their assignments because they all lived in New York City and a short subway ride away from their assigned courts. Court Officer-Trainee Barbara Beccord lived in Brooklyn and was assigned to the NYC Civil Court in Kings County (Brooklyn), at 141 Livingston Street. Her commute was less than twenty minutes. Her starting date at the court was May 16, 2019. The second Court Officer-Trainee, Bill Howard, who lived in Manhattan (New York County) was assigned to the criminal court at 80 Centre Street in Manhattan. His starting date was the same as that of Court Officer Trainee Barbara Beccord. His commute was about 30 minutes. The third Court Officer-Trainee, Paula Wykoff, lived in Staten Island (Richmond County) and was assigned to the Family Court in Richmond County. The court was just a ten minute walk from where she lived. Her starting date was May 30, 2019. The reason for this later date is that she had a previously planned vacation and had asked permission to postpone her start date.

On June 26, 2019 all three attended a training session in Manhattan. There they exchanged stories about their first experiences and continued training at their courts. Court Officer-Trainee Barbara Beccord stated that she was working in a Landlord and Tenant Trial Part. Court Officer-Trainee Bill Howard, mentioned that he was assigned to a criminal arraignment part, along with four other Court Officers. One of them was a Sergeant, Frank Springer, who supervised the other officers and made sure that the security remained high and the flow of criminal defendants proceeded efficiently. Court Officer-Trainee, Paula Wykoff, mentioned that she was assigned to a PINS Part in family court. She found her work very satisfying because the part was a strong tool in the process of guiding children who needed supervision.

They also discussed upcoming promotional exams, both in the Court Officer series and in the court clerk series. All expressed their gratitude for their fellow Court Officers and other court employees who were already encouraging them to consider participating in the promotional exam process.

Questions for passage 1 are on the following page.

Court Officer New York State (NYS Court Officer-Trainee)

Memory Passage 1:

Questions 1-10

1. Which of the following names is the correct name of one of the Court Officer-Trainees?
   A. Paul Wykofsky
   B. Paula Wykoff
   C. Paul Wiskoff
   D. Paula Wykofsky

2. The starting date of the Court Officer-Trainee assigned to Staten Island (Richmond County) is:
   A. May 30, 2019
   B. June 26, 2018
   C. April 30, 2019
   D. June 30, 2019

3. Court Officer-Trainee Barbara Beccord was assigned to:
   A. 141 Livingston Street
   B. 80 Centre Street
   C. Family Court
   D. Surrogates Court

4. The three Court Officer-Trainees attended a training session in:
   A. Brooklyn
   B. Kings County
   C. Richmond County
   D. Manhattan

5. The name of the Court Officer Sergeant is:
   A. Paul Springer
   B. Frank Beccord
   C. Paul Wykoff
   D. Frank Springer

6. The Court Officer-Trainee assigned to 141 Livingston Street lives in:
   A. New York County
   B. Manhattan
   C. Brooklyn
   D. Staten Island

7. The Court Officer-Trainee who has the longest commute is:
   A. Barbara Hazelton
   B. Bob Beccord
   C. Bill Howard
   D. James Melton

8. The Family Court part mentioned in the passage is a:
   A. JD Part
   B. DAT Part
   C. PINS Part
   D. DSE Part

9. The family court part mentioned in the passage handles children who need:
A. Probation
B. Supervision
C. Restitution
D. Confinement

10. The name of the Court-Officer Trainee who walks to work is:
A. Pauline Workof
B. Paula Wykoff
C. Paul Wikofsky
D. Paula Wiskoff

•

Answers 1-10

1. B. Paula Wykoff

2. A. May 30, 2019

3. A. 141 Livingston Street

4. D. Manhattan

5. D. Frank Springer

6. C. Brooklyn

7. C. Bill Howard

8. C. PINS Part

9. B. Supervision

10. B. Paula Wykoff

**Try practicing memory questions by reading a passage (300-400 words)
in a non-fiction book and then after 10 minutes write down as many details as you can
remember.**

The more you practice, the better you will do on this type of question.

Memory Passage 2:

Directions:

When instructed by the test monitor, turn this page over and for the next 5 minutes read the passage on the page as many times as you want. Try to memorize as many details of the passage as you can. At the end of the 5 minutes, when the test monitor instructs you to do so, stop reading and turn the page over. The test monitor will then collect this page.
(After the next 10 minutes, the test monitor will distribute the test booklets. When instructed to do so by the test monitor, open the test booklet and answer the first 10 questions in the booklet.)

On September 21, 2019, at 9:15 a.m. on Monday morning, Court Officer-Trainee Tania Newman was in her assigned Criminal Trial Part, 12B on the fourth floor, when she received a message on her radio that Judge Feinman had just reported that he was walking to his part when he witnessed a young female faint in the fourth floor public hall, near Part 12B.

Court Officer-Trainee Newman quickly informed the judge in her part, Judge Alice Gretsky, of the emergency and dashed out of the courtroom. The female was about fifty feet away from the doors of Part 12B. She was laying on the floor, and next to her was a young girl about eight years of age. Fortunately, Court Officer Mark Warner, who had worked as a certified medic prior to becoming a Court Officer, was on the scene and attempting to revive the female. Judge Barbara Tennor, who had served as a NYPD Officer for a number of years, was also assisting.

Court Officer-Trainee Newman contacted headquarters by radio and confirmed that an ambulance had been called. With Court Officer Warner and Judge Tennor attending to the female, Court Officer-Trainee Newman spoke with the young girl and learned that she was the daughter of the woman who had fainted. Fortunately, the young girl knew her father's cell number. Court Officer-Trainee Newman contacted the father, who was a block away, trying to find a parking spot.

Court Officer-Trainee Newman waited with the girl and kept her occupied as her mother regained consciousness and medics from the ambulance arrived. After examining and questioning the female, the medics stated that they suspected that she fainted due to dehydration. The nervousness of going to court and testifying as a witness had made her neglect herself, and she had not had breakfast nor drank anything that morning.

The father arrived minutes later. Everyone agreed that the incident was not life-threatening. However, they also agreed that it was prudent that the woman be transported to a nearby hospital for testing. Later that morning, Supervising Judge Matthew Connors, thanked everyone personally for their assistance.

Questions for passage 2 are on the following page.

Passage 2:

Questions 1-10

1. Which of the following is the assigned part of Judge Alice Gretsky?
   A. Part 21C
   B. Part 12D
   C. Part 2E
   D. Part 12B

2. The last name of the Court Officer who had worked as a certified medic is:
   A. Newman
   B. Connors
   C. Tennor
   D. Warner

3. The date of this incident is:
   A. November 12, 2019
   B. September 21, 2019
   C. November 12, 2019
   D. September 12, 2019

4. About how old was the young girl?
   A. 6 years old
   B. 7 years old
   C. 8 years old
   D. 9 years old

5. What is the last name of the Supervising Judge?
   A. Tennor
   B. Connors
   C. Warner
   D. Gretsky

6. The father was trying to park his car and was _____ block(s) away when contacted by the Court Officer.
   A. one
   B. two
   C. three
   D. four

7. The last name of the judge who had worked as an NYPD Officer is:
   A. Newman
   B, Connors
   C. Tennor
   D. Warner

8. The Court Officer-Trainee first received a message on her radio regarding the incident at _____.
   A. 9:00 a.m.
   B. 9:05 a.m.
   C. 9:10 a.m.
   D. 9:15 a.m.

9. Court Officer-Trainee Newman contacted _____ by radio and confirmed that an ambulance had been called.
   A. Court Officer Warner
   B. Part 12D
   C. headquarters
   D. 911

10. The day of the week that the incident occurred was:
   A. Monday
   B. Wednesday
   C. Thursday
   D. Tuesday

•

Answers 1-10

1. D. Part 12B
2. D. Warner
3. B. September 21, 2019
4. C. 8 years old
5. B. Connors
6. A. one
7. C. Tennor
8. D. 9:15 a.m.
9. C. headquarters
10. A. Monday

!

HINT

To make memorization easier, did you try grouping the names of court officers, judges, dates, times, and locations?
Court officers: Newman, Warner,
Judges: Feinman, Gretsky, Tennor, Connors
dates and times: 9/1/2019 , 9:15 a.m.
locations: 12B, 4th floor

Remember, the more you practice, the better you will do with this type of question.

Passage 3:

Directions:

When instructed by the test monitor, turn this page over and for the next 5 minutes read the passage on the page as many times as you want. Try to memorize as many details of the passage as you can. At the end of the 5 minutes, when the test monitor instructs you to do so, stop reading and turn the page over. The test monitor will then collect this page.

(After the next 10 minutes, the test monitor will distribute the test booklets. When instructed to do so by the test monitor, open the test booklet and answer the first 10 questions in the booklet.)

On October 22, 2019, at 9:00 a.m., Court Officer Juanita Hernandez and Court Officer-Trainee Anatoly Petrov reported to Landlord and Tenant courtroom 35C on the seventh floor of the NYC Civil Court, Queens County. It was the first day of Term 10. They were both new to the part, as was the Senior Court Clerk Hazel Jones and Housing Judge William Rodinsky, a newly appointed judge with many years of experience as a Landlord and Tenant attorney. They were all taking over the calendar of Housing Judge Eleanor Vaughan, who had just retired a few days earlier.

Because it was their first day working together and because they were assuming the inventory of cases from a retired judge, Supervising Judge Thomas Samuelson had ordered only an afternoon calendar of cases for the part, leaving the morning hours available for the personnel in the part to get their bearings and ensure that all the files and order forms were available.

The afternoon calendar was originally scheduled for 2:00 p.m. However, Housing Judge William Rodinsky delayed the calendar call until 3:00 p.m. Although at first both Court Officers and the Senior Court Clerk assigned to the part wondered why, they quickly understood the logic behind it. When the Senior Court Clerk called the calendar, 27 of the cases were marked "Settled" at the calendar call, with only 12 cases marked "Ready for Conference." The additional hour had allowed parties to discuss their cases and come to a large number of agreements. The number of settled cases was much more than usual and allowed for more time to conference the remaining cases. By 5:00 p.m. only two cases remained undisposed. Both cases were adjourned for trial on October 29, one week later.

Before the part adjourned for the day, the Court Officers and Senior Court Clerk reviewed the calendar for the following day. The morning calendar had 36 cases and was scheduled for 9:30 a.m. After Housing Judge Rodinsky thanked them all for the fine effort they put in during the day, he suggested that tomorrow they should allow the litigants an hour to conference together, and therefore postponed the calendar call until 10:30 a.m.

Questions for passage 3 are on the following page.

Passage 3:

Questions 1-10

1. The afternoon calendar for the day was originally scheduled for:
   A. 12:00 p.m.
   B. 1:00 p.m.
   C. 2:00 p.m.
   D. 5:00 p.m.

2. The last name of the Senior Court Clerk is:
   A. Hernandez
   B. Rodinsky
   C. Samuelson
   D. Jones

3. The number of cases marked "settled" at the calendar call in the afternoon was:
   A. 12
   B. 15
   C. 22
   D. 27

4. The last name of the Housing Judge of the Part is:
   A. Hernandez
   B. Rodinsky
   C. Samuelson
   D. Jones

5. The afternoon calendar was actually called at:
   A. 12:00 p.m.
   B. 1:00 p.m.
   C. 2:00 p.m.
   D. 3:00 p.m.

6. The number of cases marked "Ready for Conference" was:
   A. 12
   B. 15
   C. 22
   D. 27

7. The last name of the Supervising Judge is:
   A. Hernandez
   B. Rodinsky
   C. Samuelson
   D. Jones

8. The Housing Part is on which floor?
   A. second floor
   B. fourth floor
   C. sixth floor
   D. seventh floor

9. The two undisposed cases were adjourned to:
   A. October 21
   B. October 24
   C. October 29
   D. October 31

10. This passage relates events on the first day of Term____?
   A. 2
   B. 5
   C. 7
   D. 10

•

Answers 1-10

1. C. 2:00 p.m.
2. D. Jones
3. D. 27
4. B. Rodinsky
5. D. 3:00 p.m.
6. A. 12
7. C. Samuelson
8. D. seventh floor
9. C. October 29
10. D. 10

!

HINT

To make memorization easier, did you try grouping facts?
Location: Part 35C, 7 floor
Officers: Hernandez, Petrov
Clerk: Jones
Judges: Rodinsky, Vaughan, Samuelson
Number of cases: 27/12/2
Times: 9am/10am, 2pm/3pm
Dates: Oct 22/Oct 29

Remember, the more you practice, the better you will do with this type of question.

CHAPTER 7: Record Keeping

"These questions will assess your ability to read, combine and manipulate written information organized from several different sources."[1]

The information is usually presented in a series of **tables**, and the questions are **NOT** easy.

Since 1983, as far as we know, the information has been presented only in **TABLES**.

It has **NOT** been presented in pie charts, bar graphs, or line graphs.

From "Sample Examination Questions" (Office of Court Administration):
"Directions: Answer the...questions based on the information contained in the following tables. Remember, all of the information needed to answer the questions correctly can be found in the tables."

The examples on the next page are simplified examples of record keeping questions. The level of difficulty of these types of questions will be much greater on the actual exam. It will be similar to the table question in the practice exam.

A simple table:

Title of Table: Day this table refers to:	**List of Cases by Day of the Week** **Monday**		
Part (Courtroom)	**Date Filed** (Date first case papers were filed)	**Case Status** (Current status of case)	**Money Award** (Amount, if any, that was awarded)
ROW →			COLUMN ↑

Record Keeping Example 1:

	Log of Cases by Day (Day they appeared on the Part calendars) Monday		
Part	**Date Case Papers Filed**	**Status**	**Money Awarded**
Part 4	07/22/16	Adjourned	X
Part 7	09/15/16	Dismissed	X
Part 9	11/18/15	Adjourned	X
Part 7	04/13/15	Adjourned	X
Part 6	01/09/17	Settled	$2,450

"Calendar" means the list of cases that appeared in a "Part" (courtroom).
"Adjourned" means "postponed".
"Dismissed" means "the case is over and done with, either with or without a hearing or trial".
"Settled" means that "a resolution (agreement) was reached between the parties".

What can we learn by looking at the above table?

1. The table is a list of the cases on the court calendar (cases heard in different Parts (courtrooms) on Monday).

2. The first column tells us what Part (Courtroom) the case was in.

3. The second column tells us the date that the papers for the case were first filed with the clerk's office. That is the date that the court first receives notice of the new case and the date that the case information is entered into the court filing system.

4. "Status" (third column) tells us the status of the case after it appeared on Monday in front of the judge in the specified part (courtroom).

5. The "Money Awarded" column tells us that where there is an "X", no money was awarded. If an amount is stated, then that amount is the amount of money awarded in the case. You will notice that no money was awarded in cases that were adjourned or dismissed.

6. Money was awarded in the case that appeared (was heard) in Part 6. That amount is $2,450 and was the result
   of a settlement (agreement) between the parties.

Now let's look at the Log of Cases for the following day (Tuesday). It is slightly longer and has a case with the status "Defaulted" (In this instance, "defaulted" means that the party starting the case did not appear in court).

Log of Cases by Day Tuesday			
Part	**Date Case Papers Filed**	**Status**	**Money Awarded**
Part 6	03/21/15	Adjourned	X
Part 4	12/11/16	Settled	X
Part 9	07/29/17	Dismissed	X
Part 6	09/16/16	Settled	$13,500
Part 4	03/19/16	Defaulted	X
Part 7	10/03/17	Settled	$16,500
Part 4	04/15/16	Settled	$14,250
Part 9	08/26/16	Adjourned	X

What can we learn by looking at the above table?

1. The table is a list of the cases on the court calendar (cases heard in different Parts (courtrooms) on Tuesday).

2. The first column tells us what Part (Courtroom) the case was in.

3. The second column tells us the date that the papers for the case were first filed with the clerk's office.

4. "Status" (third column) tells us the status of the case after it appeared on Tuesday in front of the judge in the specified part (courtroom).

5. The "Money Awarded" column tells us that where there is an "X", no money was awarded. If an amount is stated, then that amount is the amount of money awarded in the case. You will notice that no money was awarded in cases that were adjourned or dismissed. (There is also a "settled" case where no money was awarded.) Note that instead of an "X" to indicate "no money awarded", you may see one of the following notations: "None", "No amount," "Zero," "$0," and so on.

(On the actual exam you may have four or more logs of cases (Example: Monday, Tuesday, Wednesday, Thursday, Friday), each longer than the one on this page.) Also, instead of the tables having information about cases on different days, they may have information about cases in different courts, locations, etc.

Court Officer New York State (NYS Court Officer-Trainee)

After providing you with about four logs of cases, they may provide you with tables that you will need to fill-in by using the information in the four tables. You will need these "supplementary" or "summary" tables to arrive at the answers to the questions about the information in the tables.

An example of Summary tables that may be provided is as follows:

Summary of Cases for Monday and Tuesday			
Status of Cases	**Monday**	**Tuesday**	**Total**
Adjourned	3	2	5
Defaulted			
Dismissed			
Settled - with money award			
Settled - with no money award			
Total Number of Cases			
Cases by Year Filed			
2015			
2016			
2017			
Total Number of Cases			

Notice that the above summary table is a "combined" table of the two tables displayed on the following, opposite page. The information summarized in them would be the same. Only the presentation is different. On the test, expect either presentation. The summary tables may have some of the boxes ("table cells") already filled-in. You will have to fill-in the rest, based on the original information tables that are provided.

Example of the preceding table presented as two tables:

Summary of Cases for Monday and Tuesday (By status of case)			
Status of Cases	**Monday**	**Tuesday**	**Total**
Adjourned	3	2	5
Defaulted			
Dismissed			
Settled - with money award			
Settled - with no money award			
Total Number of Cases			

Summary of Cases for Monday and Tuesday (By year filed)			
Status of Cases	**Monday**	**Tuesday**	**Total**
Cases by Year Filed			
2015			
2016			
2017			
Total Number of Cases			

The next two pages display the summary tables on this page and preceding page already filled-in (with all the summary information posted to the table).

Court Officer New York State (NYS Court Officer-Trainee)

After providing you with about four logs of cases, they may provide you with tables that you will need to fill-in by using the information in the four tables. You will need these "supplementary" or "summary" tables to arrive at the answers for the questions that they ask about the tables.

An example of Summary tables that may be provided and that <u>you</u> fill-in (based on tables on pages 62-63) is as follows:

Summary of Cases for Monday and Tuesday			
Status of Cases	**Monday**	**Tuesday**	**Total**
Adjourned	3	2	5
Defaulted	---	1	1
Dismissed	1	1	2
Settled - with money award	1	3	4
Settled - with no money award		1	1
Total Number of Cases	5	8	13
Cases by Year Filed			
2015	2	1	3
2016	2	5	7
2017	1	2	3
Total Number of Cases	5	8	13

Notice that the above summary table is a "combined" table of the two tables displayed on the following, opposite page. The information summarized in them would be the same. Only the presentation is different. On the test, expect either presentation. The summary tables may have some of the boxes ("table cells") already filled-in. You will have to fill-in the rest, based on the original information tables that are provided.

Example of the preceding table presented as two tables and filled-in:

Summary of Cases for Monday and Tuesday (By status of case)			
Status of Cases	**Monday**	**Tuesday**	**Total**
Adjourned	3	2	5
Defaulted	---	1	1
Dismissed	1	1	2
Settled - with money award	1	3	4
Settled - with no money award		1	1
Total Number of Cases	5	8	13

Summary of Cases for Monday and Tuesday (By year filed)			
Status of Cases	**Monday**	**Tuesday**	**Total**
Cases by Year Filed			
2015	2	1	3
2016	2	5	7
2017	1	2	3
Total Number of Cases	5	8	13

The following page has 10 practice questions.

Court Officer New York State (NYS Court Officer-Trainee)

Answer the following 10 questions based on the information tables "**Log of Cases by Day: Monday and Tuesday)** and the summary table which you filled-in.

NOTE: These 10 questions are relatively easy to answer because the tables are not long. On the actual test you may see four or five tables for one series of questions, and each table may contain 25 lines of information. Also, although you may answer these 10 questions simply by referring to the original two tables of information that are provided (without need to complete the summary tables), on the actual test you will need to fill-in the summary tables to efficiently and correctly answer the questions.

Questions 1-10:

1. What is the grand total number of cases for Monday and Tuesday?
A. 12   C. 14
B. 13   D. 15

2. What is the total number of cases "Settled - with money award"?
A. 1   C. 4
B. 3   D. 5

3. What is the total number of cases that were filed in 2017?
A. 1   C. 3
B. 2   D. 4

4. What is the total number of cases that were filed in 2015?
A. 1   C. 4
B. 3   D. 2

5. How many 2016 cases appeared in court on Monday?
A. 1   C. 4
B. 3   D. 2

6. What is the total number of cases that were in court on Tuesday?
A. 8   C. 7
B. 6   D. 9

7. Which year had the greatest number of cases filed?
A. 2014   C. 2016
B. 2015   D. 2017

8. What is the total number of cases "defaulted" on Monday and Tuesday.
A. 1   C. 4
B. 3   D. 2

9. Which of the following statements is correct?
A. Monday had more cases than Tuesday.
B. 2015 and 2016 had the same number of filed cases.
C. The total number of case "Settled - with money award" exceeds the number of cases "Settled - with no money award" by four.
D. The number of cases filed in 2016 is more than the total number of cases filed in 2015 and 2017.

10. The total number of cases adjourned plus the total number of cases defaulted is:
A. 6   C. 7
B. 5   D. 8

Answers 1-10:

1. B. 13
The "total number of cases for Monday and Tuesday" is the intersection of the "Total" column and the "Total Number of Cases" row.

2. C. 4
The "total number of cases "Settled - with money award" is the intersection of the "Total" column and the "Settled - with money award" row.

3. C. 3
The total number of cases that were filed in 2017 is the intersection of the "Total column" and the "2017" row.

4. B. 3
The total number of cases that were filed in 2015 is the intersection of the "Total column" and the "2015" row.

5. D. 2
The number of 2016 cases appeared in court on Monday is the intersection of the "Monday" column and the "2016" row.

6. A. 8
The "total number of cases that were in court on Tuesday" is the intersection of the "Tuesday" column and the "Total number of cases" row.

7. C. 2016
The year with the greatest number of cases filed was 2016. It had 7 cases, as compared to 2015 and 2017 which had 3 cases each.

8. A. 1
The total number of cases "defaulted" on Monday and Tuesday is the intersection of the "Total" column and the "Defaulted" row.

9. D. The number of cases filed in 2016 is more than the total number of cases filed in 2015 and 2017.
2015 cases filed: 3
2016 cases filed: 7 (greatest number of cases filed)
2017 cases filed: 3

10. A. 6
The total number of cases adjourned and defaulted is adjourned (5) plus defaulted (1) = 6

Filling-in Missing Information

On the exam, you may be provided with a table where some information is missing in one or more cells. Before you can continue with the problem, you will have to fill-in the information that is missing. For example, if you are provided with a table such as the following table (BUT ABOUT 3-4 TIMES LONGER), how would you determine what the missing information is?

Summary of Cases for Monday and Tuesday			
Status of Cases	**Monday**	**Tuesday**	**Total**
Adjourned	3	?	5
Defaulted	---	1	1
Dismissed	1	1	2
Settled - with money award	1	3	4
Settled - with no money award	---	1	?
Total Number of Cases	5	8	13
Cases by Year Filed			
2015	2	1	3
2016	2	5	7
2017	1	2	?
Total Number of Cases	5	8	13

The missing information may be indicated with a "?" mark, or a line "____" any other notation, or simply a blank space. In the example on the previous page, the missing information is indicated with a "__?__". Can you tell how we arrived at the missing numbers below (indicated in bold)?

Summary of Cases for Monday and Tuesday			
Status of Cases	**Monday**	**Tuesday**	**Total**
Adjourned	3	**2**	5
Defaulted	---	1	1
Dismissed	1	1	2
Settled - with money award	1	3	4
Settled - with no money award	---	1	**1**
Total Number of Cases	5	8	13
Cases by Year Filed			
2015	2	1	3
2016	2	5	7
2017	1	2	**3**
Total Number of Cases	5	8	13

1. The "2" in the adjourned row is determined as follows: The total adjourned is 5. On Monday 3 cases were adjourned. Therefore, on Tuesday there must have been 2 cases adjourned (3+2=5).

2. The "1" in the "Total" column is determined as follows: The total number of cases is 13 (The intersection of the "Total column and the "Total Number of Cases" row). If you add the Total for each of the other types of cases, (Adjourned 5 + Defaulted 1 + Dismissed 2 + Settled- with money award 4 = 12 cases) and subtract it from the Total number of cases (13), then the difference is "1".

3. The "3" in the "Total" column is the sum of 2017 cases on Monday (1) and Tuesday (2): 1 + 2 = 3.

Cases handled by
Judge Nicholas Vernon
June 22, 2019

FAM 29756

FAM 29757

FAM 29758

CIV 74562

CIV 74563

CRM 43867

FAM ___?___

CIV ___?___

FAM 29760

FAM ___?___

CRM ___?___

FAM 29762

CIV 74565

CRM 43869

FAM 29763

In the box on the left, there is information for a more complicated version of the "fill-in the missing numbers" type of question.

————

This example deals with Judge Nicholas Vernon, who is assigned to a small court in a rural community.

Because of the low volume of cases, Judges in that court handle a variety of cases on the same day:
CIV: Civil
CRM: Criminal, and
FAM: Family cases.

The list of cases on the left are cases that were handled by Judge Nicholas on one day, June 22, 2019.

Because these cases are appearing before the judge for the first time, the case file numbers are in strict sequential order.

Instructions:
Based on the information provided, fill-in the missing case numbers.

(Answers are on the following page.)

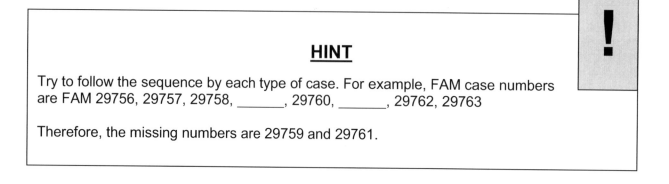

HINT

Try to follow the sequence by each type of case. For example, FAM case numbers are FAM 29756, 29757, 29758, _____, 29760, _____, 29762, 29763

Therefore, the missing numbers are 29759 and 29761.

Cases handled by
Judge Nicholas Vernon
June 22, 2019

FAM 29756

FAM 29757

FAM 29758

CIV 74562

CIV 74563

CRM 43867

FAM **29759**

CIV **74564**

FAM 29760

FAM **29761**

CRM **43868**

FAM 29762

CIV 74565

CRM 43869

FAM 29763

HINT

!

Remember that cases can be classified in many different ways:

- by type of court
  (Family Court, Civil Court, Criminal Court, Surrogates Court, etc.)

- by type of cases within a court
  (Family court: JD Proceeding, PINS, Family Offense, tec.)

- by type of criminal offense
  (Felony, misdemeanor, violation, VTL, etc.)

- by type of code
  (Code 306, Code 442, Code 517, etc.)

Whatever the classification or coding, the list will be in a logical order, with enough information provided for you to be able to determine the missing information based on logic.

The "trick" to this type of question is to be aware that it is a type of question that is asked, and also the variations in the way that it can be asked. As with all studying, practice is often the key to success.

Beginning on the following page there is a longer and more "test-type" table question.

Notice the:
1. longer tables
2. missing information that must be filled-in

Keep in mind that although only 10-15 questions may be on tables, they require a longer time to answer than other questions and are crucial in obtaining a score of 90+.

Question 1 Directions: The following table lists cases that were on the intake calendars on one day in a small city court and include civil cases, family offense cases, criminal cases, Landlord and Tenant and Small Claims cases. The cases appear on the calendar by index number order of their files. (CIV = Civil Court case, FAM = Family Court case, CRIM = Criminal Court case, SC = Small Claims case, and LT = Landlord and Tenant case.) Fill-in any missing information, complete the two summary tables that follow this table, then answer the 10 questions about the table.

Note: Money is awarded only in Civil and Small Claims cases. Fines are imposed only in criminal courts. Referrals to JD Parts are made only in Family court cases.

LIST OF CASES JUNE 26, 2019						
Case Type	Case Number	Case Filed Date	Case Status	Money Award	Fine	Referred to JD Part
CIV	2458/17	8/16/17	Settled	$4,000	---	---
FAM	5210/19	3/21/19	Hearing Completed	---	---	YES
FAM	5211/19	3/21/19	Hearing Completed	---	---	---
CRIM	6421/18	4/12/18	Trial Completed	---	$600	---
CIV	2459/17	8/16/17	Dismissed	---	---	---
LT	3617/19	5/11/19	Settled	---	---	---
SC	1524/19	4/30/19	Settled	$750	---	---
SC	1525/19	4/30/19	Defaulted	---	---	---
LT	--- 1? ---	5/12/19	Adjourned	---	---	---
FAM	5212/19	3/22/19	Dismissed	---	---	---
CRIM	6422/18	4/12/18	Adjourned	---	---	---
CIV	2460/17	8/16/17	Defaulted	---	---	---
--- 2? ---	5213/19	3/22/19	Hearing Completed	---	---	---
SC	1526/19	5/1/19	Settled	$980	---	---
LT	3619/19	5/12/19	Adjourned	---	---	---
CIV	2461/17	8/17/17	Settled	$5,750	---	---
CIV	2462/17	8/17/17	Settled	---	---	---
LT	3620/19	5/13/19	Dismissed	---	---	---
--- 3 ?---	1527/19	5/19/19	Dismissed	---	---	---
FAM	5214/19	3/24/19	Hearing Completed	---	---	YES
CRIM	6423/18	4/13/18	Trial Completed	---	$1,250	---
CRIM	6424/18	4/13/18	Dismissed	---	---	---

LIST OF CASES (cont'd) JUNE 26, 2019						
Case Type	Case Number	Case Filed Date	Case Status	Money Award	Fine	Referred to JD Part
LT	3621/19	5/19/19	Adjourned	---	---	---
CIV	2463/17	8/18/17	Settled	$4,900	---	---
FAM	5215/19	3/25/19	Hearing Completed	---	---	---
CIV	2464/17	8/18/17	Defaulted	---	---	---
SC	1528/19	5/20/19	Settled	$3,500	---	---
LT	3622/19	5/19/19	Dismissed	---	---	---
CRIM	6425/18	4/13/18	Trial Completed	---	$4,000	---

COURT CODES		
Court	**Case Type**	**Number Code**
Family Court	FAM	1
Criminal Court	CRIM	2
Civil Court	CIV	3
Landlord and Tenant Court	LT	4
Small Claims Court	SC	5

Two summary tables are on the next page.

CASES ON CALENDAR JUNE 26, 2019
CODES 1-5

Case Result	Code 1	Code 2	Code 3	Code 4	Code 5	Total Cases
Dismissed						
Defaulted						
Adjourned						
Hearing Completed (Referred to JD Part or not Referred to JD Part)						
Trial Completed - with fine						
Trial completed - with no fine						
Settled - with no money award						
Settled - with money award						
Total Cases						

CASES ON CALENDAR JUNE 26, 2019
YEAR FILED

Year Filed	Code 1	Code 2	Code 3	Code 4	Code 5	Total Cases
2017						
2018						
2019						
Total Cases						

Before we try to answer questions, let's discuss the BEST (most correct and efficient) way to fill-in the information in the summary tables. The summary table "**CASES ON CALENDAR JUNE 26, 2019**" has 40 cells (plus the "Total" cells) that need to be filled-in. This should not be difficult to do, since all that is needed is to count the items in the main table that fit into each cell in the summary table. HOWEVER, since we are limited in time, we have to use the most <u>efficient</u> method.

HINT

Method 1: (<u>**NOT**</u> a good method)

We determine what information is needed for each cell in the summary table and then go down the main table and count those items.
By using this method, we have to go down the main table and count the items 40 times (once for each cell in the summary table).

Method 2: **(THE BEST METHOD)**

WE START WITH ROW 1 IN THE MAIN TABLE AND DETERMINE WHAT INFORMATION SHOULD BE POSTED IN THE SUMMARY TABLE.

AFTER ROW ONE, WE GO TO ROW 2 AND DETERMINE WHAT INFORMATION SHOULD BE POSTED IN THE SUMMARY TABLE.

AFTER ROW TWO, WE GO TO ROW 3. ETC., UNTIL WE HAVE GONE DOWN ALL THE ROWS OF THE TABLE.

By using this method, we go down the main table, row after row (8 rows), and count the items eight times instead of 40 times. A **BIG** TIME SAVER.

NOTE: The most common remark that we hear from test-takers is that they "did not have enough time" to finish the exam. Beware of the time needed for table questions. We suggest that you practice and become proficient in these questions by using Method 2.

Another common complaint is that it is difficult to "post" information in the summary tables because the main table and the summary table are often on different pages of the test booklet.
After posting to the summary table, it is sometimes easy to lose track of the last line (row) that was posted from the main table. Candidates report that they have sometimes skipped a line or posted it twice.
To prevent this, place a check mark " ✔ " on the row in the main table after you are finished with it. (See pages 84 - 86.)

HINT

Question: If you were provided with the preceding "List of Cases" table, what would be the first thing that you would need to do?

Answer: Determine what information should go in the blank cells marked 1?, 2?, and 3?.

Also, you should notice that the "Case Type" in the "COURT CODES" table have Number Codes. This probably indicates that the "Court", "Case Type" and "Number Codes" will probably be necessary to answer questions about the tables.

You will notice that "Case Type' is the title of the first column of the main table. However, "Case Type" is not anywhere in the summary tables. Instead of "Case Type," the Code for each case type is listed in the summary tables. To match the "Case Type" to the Code, write-in the Code for each "Case Type" next to each case type in column one of the main table. (See page 80 and 81.)

Directions:

Answer the following 10 questions based on the preceding "List of Cases" table, "List of Codes" table, and two summary tables that you filled-in.

1. Which of the following is a logical replacement for "--- 1? ---" in the cell in the "Case Number" column of the "List of Cases" table?
A. 3617/19   C. 3618/19
B. 3618/18   D. 3617/17

2. Which of the following is a logical replacement for "--- 2? ---"?
A. CRIM   C. LT
B. CIV   D. FAM

3. What is the total number of cases on the calendar minus the total number of defaulted cases?
A. 24   C. 26
B. 25   D. 27

4. What is the total number of "Hearing Completed" cases?
A. 4   C. 3
B. 5   D. 6

5. The total number of cases "Settled - with money award" exceeds the total number of cases "Settled - with no money award" by:
A. 4   C. 3
B. 5   D. 6

6. What is the total of Code 2 and Code 3 cases?

A. 10   C. 14

B. 12   D. 16

7. How many cases were filed in 2017?

A. 7   C. 5

B. 8   D. 6

8. The number of cases filed in 2019 exceeds the number of cases file in 2018 by:

A. 10   C. 14

B. 13   D. 12

9. What is the total number of Code 1 and Code 2 cases?

A. 10   C. 14

B. 11   D. 12

10. The number of case of Case type "FAM" plus the number of cases of Case type "CRIM" is:

A. 10   C. 14

B. 11   D. 12

Court Officer New York State (NYS Court Officer-Trainee)

The following Main Table and two summary tables include notations that we mentioned.

	LIST OF CASES JUNE 26, 2019					
Case Type	Case Number	Case Filed Date	Case Status	Money Award	Fine	Referred to JD Part
3 CIV ✔ ✔	2458/17	8/16/17	Settled	$4,000	---	---
1 FAM ✔ ✔	5210/19	3/21/19	Hearing Completed	---	---	YES
1 FAM ✔ ✔	5211/19	3/21/19	Hearing Completed	---	---	---
2 CRIM ✔ ✔	6421/18	4/12/18	Trial Completed	---	$600	---
3 CIV ✔ ✔	2459/17	8/16/17	Dismissed	---	---	---
4 LT ✔ ✔	3617/19	5/11/19	Settled	---	---	---
5 SC ✔ ✔	1524/19	4/30/19	Settled	$750	---	---
5 SC ✔ ✔	1525/19	4/30/19	Defaulted	---	---	---
4 LT ✔ ✔	*3618/19*	5/12/19	Adjourned	---	---	---
1 FAM ✔ ✔	5212/19	3/22/19	Dismissed	---	---	---
2 CRIM ✔ ✔	6422/18	4/12/18	Adjourned	---	---	---
3 CIV ✔ ✔	2460/17	8/16/17	Defaulted	---	---	---
1 *FAM* ✔ ✔	5213/19	3/22/19	Hearing Completed	---	---	---
5 SC ✔ ✔	1526/19	5/1/19	Settled	$980	---	---
4 LT ✔ ✔	3619/19	5/12/19	Adjourned	---	---	---
3 CIV ✔ ✔	2461/17	8/17/17	Settled	$5,750	---	---
3 CIV ✔ ✔	2462/17	8/17/17	Settled	---	---	---
4 LT ✔ ✔	3620/19	5/13/19	Dismissed	---	---	---
5 *SC* ✔ ✔	1527/19	5/19/19	Dismissed	---	---	---
1 FAM ✔ ✔	5214/19	3/24/19	Hearing Completed	---	---	YES
2 CRIM ✔ ✔	6423/18	4/13/18	Trial Completed	---	$1,250	---
2 CRIM ✔ ✔	6424/18	4/13/18	Dismissed	---	---	---

84

LIST OF CASES (cont'd) JUNE 26, 2019						
Case Type	Case Number	Case Filed Date	Case Status	Money Award	Fine	Referred to JD Part
4 LT ✔ ✔	3621/19	5/19/19	Adjourned	---	---	---
3 CIV ✔ ✔	2463/17	8/18/17	Settled	$4,900	---	---
1 FAM ✔ ✔	5215/19	3/25/19	Hearing Completed	---	---	---
3 CIV ✔ ✔	2464/17	8/18/17	Defaulted	---	---	---
5 SC ✔ ✔	1528/19	5/20/19	Settled	$3,500	---	---
4 LT ✔ ✔	3622/19	5/19/19	Dismissed	---	---	---
2 CRIM ✔ ✔	6425/18	4/13/18	Trial Completed	---	$4,000	---

CASES ON CALENDAR JUNE 26, 2019 YEAR FILED						
Year Filed	Code 1	Code 2	Code 3	Code 4	Code 5	Total Cases
2017			7 ///////			7
2018		5 /////				5
2019	6 ///////			6 //////	5 /////	17
Total Cases	6	5	7	6	5	29

CASES ON CALENDAR JUNE 26, 2019 CODES 1-5						
Case Result	Code 1	Code 2	Code 3	Code 4	Code 5	Total Cases
Dismissed	/ 1	/ 1	/ 1	// 2	/ 1	6
Defaulted			// 2		/ 1	3
Adjourned		/ 1		/// 3		4
Hearing Completed (Referred to JD Part or not Referred to JD Part)	///// 5					5
Trial Completed - with fine		/// 3				3
Trial completed - with no fine						
Settled - with no money award			/ 1	/ 1		2
Settled - with money award			/// 3		/// 3	6
Total Cases	6	5	7	6	5	29

Answers 1-10

1. Which of the following is a logical replacement for "--- 1? ---" in the cell in the "Case Number" column of the "List of Cases" Table?

A. 3617/19

B. 3618/18

C. 3618/19

D. 3617/17

The previous Code 4 case number on the list was 3617/19, therefore this Code 4 case number must be 3618/19 because the case numbers within each code are sequential.

2. Which of the following is a logical replacement for "--- 2? ---"?

A. CRIM
B. CIV
C. LT
D. FAM

The case number in the row where the "--- 2? ---"? is located is 5213/19. If we look at the list, case number 5212/19 is a FAM case. Therefore a correct replacement is "FAM".

3. What is the total number of cases on the calendar minus the total number of defaulted cases?

A. 24
B. 25
C. 26
D. 27

Total cases (29) from the intersection of "Total Cases" column and "Total Cases" row on the summary table "CASES ON CALENDAR JUNE 26, 2019" minus the total defaulted cases (3) = 26.

4. What is the total number of "Hearing Completed" cases?

A. 4
B. 5
C. 3
D. 6

From the summary table "CASES ON CALENDAR JUNE 26, 2019" (intersection of "total cases" column and "Hearing Completed" cases.

5. The total number of cases "Settled - with money award" exceeds the total number of cases "Settled - with no money award" by:

A. 4
B. 5
C. 3
D. 6

From the summary table "CASES ON CALENDAR JUNE 26, 2019" "Total cases" column: (6) - (2) = 4.

6. What is the total of Code 2 and Code 3 cases?

A. 10
B. 12
C. 14
D. 16

From the summary table "CASES ON CALENDAR JUNE 26, 2019" Total cases for Code 2 and 3 columns: (5) + (7) = 12.

7. How many cases were filed in 2017?

A. 7
B. 8
C. 5
D. 6

From the summary table "CASES ON CALENDAR JUNE 26, 2019 YEAR FILED", intersection of "Total Cases" column and "2017" row.

8. The number of cases filed in 2019 exceeds the number of cases file in 2018 by:

A. 10
B. 13
C. 14
D. 12

From the summary table "CASES ON CALENDAR JUNE 26, 2019 YEAR FILED", intersection of "Total Cases" column and "2019" row (17 cases) less the intersection of "Total Cases" column and "2018" row (5) = 12.

9. What is the total number of Code 1 and Code 2 cases?

A. 10   C. 14

B. 11   D. 12

The total of Code 1 and Code 2 columns in both summary tables: (6) + (5) = 11.

10. The number of case of Case type "FAM" plus the number of cases of Case type "CRIM" is:

A. 10   C. 14

B. 11   D. 12

The total of Code 1 (FAM) and Code 2 (CRIM) columns in both summary tables: (6) + (5) = 11.

A 70-Question Practice Test starts on the next page.

Try to complete the test in one sitting (maximum 3 hours). This will give you a good idea about how fast you will need to go on the actual exam to finish during the allotted time.

Concentrate on efficiently answering the table questions. Remember that these questions take longer to answer than the other questions on the exam. Although on the test these table questions might only total 10-15 questions, you will need to do your best on them to score high so that you will become a Court Officer as soon as possible.

Good Luck!

PRACTICE TEST
70 QUESTIONS

Clerical Checking

Instructions: Questions 1-10 (below) consist of three sets of information. Compare the information in each set and mark your answer sheet, as follows:

Mark: Choice A if all three sets are exactly alike

Choice B if none of the three sets are exactly alike.

Choice C if only the second and third sets are exactly alike

Choice D if only the first and second sets are exactly alike

---

1. 897454-237852 KCV-26
   Rooms 8132, 4859, 6031
   SCPA 4052 and CPL 4491
   5/18/18, 7/13/20, 8/1/21
   8743 Farmers Drive, (NY)

2. Sgt. John Boulderman, Jr.
   Court Int. Grace Kravitz
   Witness: Nancy Ann Ecker
   Summary Rep. 6912: 5 Folio
   G: 4857834-292 (Series L-B)

3. Social Services DK-21949
   Court Reporter Samsoned
   Judge Richard Wescott Sr.
   Priority (MS-2-5893439354)
   Gugenheim and Bakersville

4. MOH: 4/21/19, 11/25/19
   Kings, NY 11275-2267
   Seq. Ref.: Q-317-51362
   Leiman Briskol (Oswego)
   557 Bay Parkway, 2nd floor

5. FCA Section 3028(c) (2018)
   Court Assistant Overman
   ID # 4649517566-750-2018
   221800-B Vanders Highway
   Leonard Harrison, ID: H-3238

6. 225 S. Beachgate, NJ
   Evidence and Records Dept.
   Judge David M. Faulkner
   Req. #:2547/2018 (Neiman)
   Sealed file R:38972/2019

1. 897454-237852 KCV-26
   Rooms 8132, 4859, 6031
   SCPA 4052 and CPL 4491
   5/18/18, 7/13/20, 8/1/21
   8743 Farmers Drive, (NY)

2. Sgt. John Boulderman, Jr.
   Court Int. Grace Kravits
   Witness: Nancy Ann Ecker
   Summary Rep. 6912: 5 Folio
   G: 4857834-292 (Series L-B)

3. Social Services DK-21949
   Court Reporter Samsoned
   Judge Richard Wescott Sr.
   Priority (MS-2-5893439354)
   Gugenheim and Bakersville

4. MOH: 4/21/19, 11/25/19
   Kings, NY 11275-2267
   Seq. Ref.: Q-317-51362
   Leiman Briskoll (Oswego)
   557 Bay Parkway, 2nd floor

5. FCA Section 3028(e) (2018)
   Court Assistant Overman
   ID # 4649517566-750-2018
   221800-B Vander Highway
   Leonard Harrison, ID: H-3238

6. 225 S. Beachgate, NJ
   Evidence and Records Dept.
   Judge David M. Faulkner
   Req. #:2547/2018 (Neiman)
   Sealed file R:38972/2019

1. 897454-237852 KCV-26
   Rooms 8132, 4859, 6031
   SCPA 4052 and CPL 4491
   5/18/18, 7/13/20, 8/1/21
   8743 Farmers Drive, (NY)

2. Sgt. John Bouldermen, Jr.
   Court Int. Grace Kravitz
   Witness: Nancy Ann Ecker
   Summary Rep. 6912: 5 Folio
   G: 4857834-292 (Series L-B)

3. Social Services DK-21949
   Court Reporter Samsoned
   Judge Richard Wescott Sr.
   Priority (MS-2-5893439854)
   Gugenheim and Bakersville

4. MOH: 4/21/19, 11/25/19
   Kings, NY 11275-2267
   Seq. Ref.: Q-317-51362
   Leiman Briskoll (Oswego)
   557 Bay Parkway, 2nd floor

5. FCA Section 3028(e) (2018)
   Court Assistant Overman
   ID # 4649517566-750-2018
   221800-B Vanders Highway
   Leonard Harrison, ID: H-3238

6. 225 S. Beachgate, NJ
   Evidence and Records Dept.
   Judge David M. Faulkner
   Req. #:2547/2018 (Nieman)
   Sealed file R:38972/2019

7. Kermini, Samuel (Family Ct.)
(267) 432-1548 (8 a.m.)
Outerbanks, NJ, 20236
142-50 S. Jersey Highway
Examiner Lyndon Rockerfeller

8. Happy Vally, NY 12739-2428
Nervana Circle 12683-9758
Justice Luke Wortman-Ellis
ID: 263214853-73599326
Reg. 3059/D-254 (e) and (g)

9. Harmon, Spelling, & Jones
Civil Court Pub. 2019-12P
1832 Marmon St., Suite 5
New York, NY 10032-2366
ID #: 486452-2018 (F)

10. Brooklyn, NY 11229-6017
CR Benjamin F. Bowman
2743-02-5208 and 872-36
Rooms (502), (5498), (9781)
SCPA 2019 (Section 1065)

7. Kermini, Samuel (Family Ct.)
(267) 432-1548 (8 a.m.)
Outerbanks, NJ, 20236
142-50 S. Jersey Highway
Examiner Lyndon Rockerfeller

8. Happy Valley, NY 12739-2428
Nervana Circle 12683-9758
Justice Luke Wortman-Ellis
ID: 263214853-73599326
Reg. 3059/D-254 (e) and (g)

9. Harmon, Spelling, & Jones
Civil Court Pub. 2019-12P
1832 Marmon St., Suite 5
New York, NY 10032-2366
ID #: 486452-2018 (F)

10. Brooklyn, NY 11259-6017
CR Benjamin F. Bowmen
2743-02-5208 and 872-36
Rooms (502), (5498), (9781)
SCPA 2019 (Section 1065)

7. Kermini, Samuel (Family Ct.)
(267) 432-1548 (8 a.m.)
Outerbanks, NJ, 20236
142-50 S. Jersey Highway
Examiner Lyndon Rockefeller

8. Happy Valley, NY 12739-2428
Nervana Circle 12683-9758
Justice Luke Wortman-Ellis
ID: 263214853-73599326
Reg. 3059/D-254 (e) and (g)

9. Harmon, Spelling, & Jones
Civil Court Pub. 2019-12P
1832 Marmon St., Suite 5
New York, NY 10032-2366
ID #: 486452-2018 (F)

10. Brooklyn, NY 11259-6017
CR Benjamin F. Bowman
2743-02-5208 and 872-36
Rooms (502), (5498), (9781)
SCPA 2019 (Section 1065)

Instructions; Questions 11-20 (below) consist of three sets of information. Compare the information in each set and mark your answer sheet, as follows:
A. Only the second and third sets are exactly alike
B. Only the first and second sets are exactly alike
C. None of the sets are exactly alike
D. All three sets are exactly alike

11. 42565933922-4806
Specter Street, NJ
James Albert Wayings
Assault, second degree
Kevin F. Bromowitz

12. 427354-348967 COS3-2
Suites 5625, 3855, 7035
CPLR 1102 and CPL 44427
4/21/18, 6/12/19, 12/3/19
57472 Taylor Circle, (NJ)

13. Sgt. Gill Borman, Jr.
Sayville: J. Edmont, Sn.
George V. Mantions, Jr.
CV Numb. 3957: (3865348)
N: 1693952-2528 (Ser. K-N)

11. 42565933922-4806
Specter Street, NJ
James Albert Wayings
Assault, second degree
Kevin F. Bromowitz

12. 427354-348967 COS3-2
Suites 5625, 3855, 7035
CPLR 1102 and CPL 44427
4/21/18, 6/12/19, 12/3/19
57472 Taylor Circle, (NJ)

13. Sgt. Gill Borman, Jr.
Sayville: J. Edmont, Sn.
George V. Mantions, Jr.
CV Numb. 3957: (3865348)
N: 1693952-2928 (Ser. K-N)

11. 42565933952-4806
Specter Street, NJ
James Albert Wayings
Assault, second degree
Kevin F. Bromowitz

12. 427354-348967 COS3-2
Suites 5625, 3855, 7035
CPLR 1102 and CPL 4427
4/21/18, 6/12/19, 12/3/19
57472 Taylor Circle, (NJ)

13. Sgt. Jill Borman, Jr.
Sayville: J. Edmont, Sn.
George V. Mantions, Jr.
CV Numb. 3957: (3865348)
N: 1693952-2528 (Ser. K-N)

Court Officer New York State (NYS Court Officer-Trainee)

14. Inc. Report SSN 2809237
Junior Clerk L. Simons
CO - Lawrence Washington
Vol. (SDK-2 - 3869764-4392)
Cloverfield and Lawtonfille 3

15. Beacon, NY 11508-2673
JHO Nancy Heatherfield
422-37-7243 and 4285-58
Rooms (404-A), (659 -CB)
Appellate Division, 2 Dept.

16. Wernor Junction, NJ 07039
Seaton Lane (West 315657)
Judge Saverio Appertino
ID: 386842254-75239656
Reg. 6039/D-853 (xw) and (d)

17. Furlow, Brandenstin, Rogers
Criminal Procedure Law
73-49 Heathurs Boulevard
Yonkers, NY 10732-3295
Ref. #: 6895252-1579 (B-D)

18. 30953392-398494 SAR-525
Supply Rms. 369, 8825, 7037
EPT 301(c) & CPL 6224(d)
9/2/18, 9/9/19, 5/8/19, 6/7/19
7742 Darwin Avenue, (CT)

19. Sgt. Solomon Beckers-Chin
Ct. Off. Sgt. Maria Latnova
Ct. Rep. Mohamed Ayman
UIR 799735: 9 Series K-M
G: 9697974-336 (Series E-P)

20. Daily W-234468148959
Ct. Officer J. Lumowitz, Sr.
Magistrate M. J. Ermington
Seq. (ABDS 2 - 487023841)
Mohamed Alvarez: 3735822

14. Inc. Report SSN 2809237
Junior Clerk L. Simons
CO - Lawrence Washington
Vol. (SDK-2 - 3869764-4392)
Cloverfield and Lawtonfille 3

15. Beacon, NY 11508-2673
JHO Nancy Heatherfield
422-37-7243 and 4285-58
Rooms (404-A), (659 -CB)
Appellate Division, 2 Dept.

16. Wernor Junction, NY 07039
Seaton Lane (West 315657)
Judge Saverio Appertino
ID: 386842254-75239656
Reg. 6039/D-853 (xw) and (d)

17. Furlow, Brandenstin, Rogers
Criminal Procedure Law
73-49 Heathers Boulevard
Yonkers, NY 10732-3295
Ref. #: 6895252-1579 (B-D)

18. 30953392-398494 SAR-525
Supply Rms. 369, 8825, 7037
EPT 301(c) & CPL 6224(d)
9/2/18, 9/9/19, 5/8/19, 6/7/19
7742 Darwin Avenue, (CT)

19. Sgt. Solomon Beckers-Chin
Ct. Off. Sgt. Maria Latnova
Ct. Rep. Mohamed Ayman
UIR 799735: 9 Series K-M
G: 9697974-336 (Series E-P)

20. Daily W-234468148929
Ct. Officer J. Lumowits, Sr.
Magistrate M. J. Ermington
Seq. (ABDS 2 - 487023841)
Mohamed Alvarez: 3735822

14. Inc. Report SSN 2809237
Junior Clerk L. Simons
CO - Lawrence Washington
Vol. (SDK-2 - 3869764-4392)
Cloverfield and Lawtonfille 3

15. Beacon, NY 11508-2673
JHO Nancy Heatherfield
422-37-7243 and 4285-58
Rooms (404-A), (659 -CB)
Appellate Division, 2 Dept.

16. Wernor Junction, NJ 07039
Seaton Lane (West 315657)
Judge Saverio Appertino
ID: 386842254-75239656
Reg. 6039/D-853 (xy) and (d)

17. Furlow, Brandenstin, Rogers
Criminal Procedure Law
73-49 Heathers Boulevard
Yonkers, NY 10732-3295
Ref. #: 6895252-1579 (B-D)

18. 30953392-398494 SAR-525
Supply Rms. 369, 8825, 7037
EPT 301(c) & CPL6224(d)
9/2/18, 9/9/19, 5/8/19, 6/7/15
7742 Darwin Avenue, (CT)

19. Sgt. Solomon Beckers-Chin
Ct. Off. Sgt. Maria Latnova
Ct. Rep. Mohamed Ayman
UIR 799735: 9 Series K-M
G: 9697974-336 (Series E-P)

20. Daily W-234468148929
Ct. Officer J. Lumowitz, Sr.
Magistrate M. J. Ermington
Seq. (ABDS 2 - 487023841)
Mohamed Alvarez: 3735822

<u>Reading and Understanding Written Material</u>

Format A: Understanding the content of a written passage

For the following questions (21-25) read the passage and then answer the question based solely on the information provided in the passage.

21. "Smoking bans are enacted in an attempt to protect people from the effects of second-hand smoke, which include an increased risk of heart disease, cancer, emphysema, and other diseases. Laws implementing bans on indoor smoking have been introduced by many countries in various forms over the years, with some legislators citing scientific evidence that shows tobacco smoking is harmful to the smokers themselves and to those inhaling second-hand smoke. In addition such laws may reduce health care costs, improve work productivity, and lower the overall cost of labor in the community thus protected, making that workforce more attractive for employers. In the US state of Indiana, the economic development agency included in its 2006 plan for acceleration of economic growth encouragement for cities and towns to adopt local smoking bans as a means of promoting job growth in communities."[4]

21. According to the above passage:
A. Illinois is a U.S. state.
B. Laws implementing bans on outdoor smoking have been introduced by many countries.
C. The US government economic development agency included in its 2006 plan for acceleration of economic growth encouragement for promoting job growth.
D. An effect of second-hand smoke is increased risk of emphysema.

•

22. "Many in the United States use the word bailiff colloquially to refer to a peace officer providing court security. More often, these Court Officers are sheriff's deputies, marshals, corrections officers or constables. The terminology varies among (and sometimes within) the several states. In rural areas, this responsibility is often carried out by the junior lawyer in training under the judge's supervision called a law clerk who also has the title of bailiff. Whatever the name used, the agency providing court security is often charged with serving legal process and seizing and selling property (e.g., replevin or foreclosure). In some cases, the duties are separated between agencies in a given jurisdiction. For instance, a Court Officer may provide courtroom security in a jurisdiction where a sheriff or constable handles service of process and seizures....In the New York State Unified Court System, Court Officers, are responsible for providing security and enforcing the law in and around court houses. Under New York State penal code, they are classified as "peace officers." New York State Court Officers are able to carry firearms both on and off duty, and have the power to make warrantless arrests both on and off duty anywhere in the State of New York. They also have the authority to make traffic stops."[4]

22. According to the above passage, which of the following four choices is correct?
A. In New York State, Court Officers are police officers.
B. A New York State Court Officer may make arrests in any part of New York State.
C. NYS Court Officers may only carry a gun while on duty.
D. Court Officers do not have authority to make traffic stops.

•

23. "Preponderance of the evidence, also known as balance of probabilities, is the standard required in most civil cases and in family court determinations solely involving money, such as child support under the Child Support Standards Act. It is also the burden of proof of which the defendant must prove affirmative defenses or mitigating circumstances in civil or criminal court. In civil court, aggravating circumstances also only have to be proven by a preponderance of the evidence, as opposed to beyond reasonable doubt (as they do in criminal court). The standard is met if the

proposition is more likely to be true than not true. The standard is satisfied if there is greater than fifty percent chance that the proposition is true. Lord Denning, in Miller v. Minister of Pensions, described it simply as "more probable than not." Until 1970, this was also the standard used in juvenile court in the United States. This is also the standard of proof used when determining eligibility of unemployment benefits for a former employee accused of losing the job through alleged misconduct. In most US states, the employer must prove this case with a preponderance of evidence. Preponderance of the evidence is the standard of proof used for immunity from prosecution under Florida's controversial stand-your-ground law. The defense must present its evidence in a pre-trial hearing, show that the statutory prerequisites have been met, and then request that the court grant a motion for declaration of immunity. The judge must then decide from the preponderance of the evidence whether to grant immunity. This is a far lower burden than "beyond a reasonable doubt," the threshold a prosecutor must meet at any proceeding criminal trial, but higher than the "probable cause" threshold generally required for indictment."(4)

23 Based on the above passage, which of the following four statements is not correct?
A. "Beyond a reasonable doubt," is a lower burden than "preponderance of the evidence."
B. "Preponderance of the evidence" is the standard of proof used for immunity from prosecution under Florida's controversial stand-your-ground law.
C. "Preponderance of the evidence" is satisfied if there is greater than fifty percent chance that the proposition is true.
D. "Preponderance of the evidence" standard is the required standard in most civil cases and in family court determinations solely involving money.

•

24. "A defined benefit pension plan is a type of pension plan in which an employer/sponsor promises a specified pension payment, lump-sum (or combination thereof) on retirement that is predetermined by a formula based on the employee's earnings history, tenure of service and age, rather than depending directly on individual investment returns. Traditionally, many governmental and public entities, as well as a large number of corporations, provided defined benefit plans, sometimes as a means of compensating workers in lieu of increased pay. A defined benefit plan is 'defined' in the sense that the benefit formula is defined and known in advance. Conversely, for a "defined contribution retirement saving plan", the formula for computing the employer's and employee's contributions is defined and known in advance, but the benefit to be paid out is not known in advance...When participating in a defined benefit pension plan, an employer/sponsor promises to pay the employees/members a specific benefit for life beginning at retirement. The benefit is calculated in advance using a formula based on age, earnings, and years of service. In the United States, the maximum retirement benefit permitted in 2014 under a defined benefit plan is $210,000 (up from $205,000 in 2013). Defined benefit pension plans in the U.S. currently do not have contribution limits."(4)

24. According to the above passage, which of the following four statements is not correct?
A. Defined benefit pension plans in the U.S. currently do not have contribution limits.
B. In a defined benefit plan, the benefit formula is known in advance.
C. An employer/sponsor promises to pay the employees/members a specific benefit for life beginning at the age of 62.
D. Many governmental entities provide defined benefit plans.

•

25. "Crowd control is a public security practice where large crowds are managed to prevent the outbreak of crowd crushes, affray, fights involving drunk and disorderly people or riots. Crowd crushes in particular can cause many hundreds of fatalities. Effective crowd management is about managing expected and unexpected crowd occurrences. Crowd control can involve privately hired security guards as well as police officers. Crowd control is often used at large, public gatherings like street

fairs, music festivals, stadiums and public demonstrations. At some events, security guards and police use metal detectors and sniffer dogs to prevent weapons and drugs being brought into a venue....Materials such as stanchions, crowd control barriers, fences and decals painted on the ground can be used to direct a crowd. A common method of crowd control is to use high visibility fencing to divert and corral pedestrian traffic to safety when there is any potential threat for danger. Keeping the crowd comfortable and relaxed is also essential, so things like awnings, cooling fans (in hot weather), and entertainment are sometimes used as well."(4)

25. According to the above passage, which of the following four statements is not correct?
A. Preventing fights involving drunks is a part of crowd control.
B. Sniffer dogs are used to prevent weapons from being brought into a location.
C. Because of the risk of violence, only police officers are used to effectively manage crowds.
D. Cooling fans may be used to manage crowds.

Format B: Select the best alternative from four alternatives that best completes a sentence or passage.

Directions: (Questions 26 - 35) This section contains two passages. In each passage five words or phrases have been omitted. For each omitted word, select the one word or phrase from the four alternatives that best completes the passage.

Passage 1:
Court Officer-Trainees learn a great deal at the Court Officers Academy. However, they also learn many things thereafter. Much of this later learning comes from ___26___ received from their fellow Court Officers. One of the key suggestions offered by experienced officers is to constantly ___27___ good judgment instead of being ___28___ by rules which in many cases do not apply in every situation. For example, although a "No drinks allowed" sign may be posted on the wall, there may be cases where litigants (such as persons with diabetes) should be allowed to have a water bottle. ___29___ generally known that diabetics are ___30___ to dehydration and therefore must drink water as needed.

26. a. adviser	27. a. exorcise	28. a. indulged	29. a. His	30. a. suceptable
b. advize	b. exsercise	b. constrained	b. Its'	b. susceptible
c. advise	c. exercise	c. freed	c. Its	c. impervious
d. advice	d. excorcise	d. declined	d. It's	d. immune

Passage 2:
"Diligent behavior is indicative of a work ethic; a belief that work is good in itself. Diligence is carefulness and persistent effort or work... Some ___31___ suggest diligence in a student is defined as an effort he or she puts towards balanced and ___32___ development in mental, physical, social and spiritual dimensions. They find diligence in students ___33___ correlated with academic performance. This is especially found in younger students. The support of parents and educators encourages students to be ___34___. Other factors which encourage diligence in students include motivation, discipline, concentration, responsibility and devotedness...Due diligence is the necessary amount of diligence required in a professional activity to avoid being negligent. This commonly arises in major acquisitions where the legal ___35___ of caveat emptor ("let the buyer beware") requires the purchaser to make a diligent survey of the property or service being sold."(4)

31. a. body	32. a. hollistic	33. a. are	4 a. indigent	35. a. cavat
b. person	b. holistic	b. haven't	b. diligent	b. principal
c. individual	c. holistick	c. weren't	c. indilligent	c. ambiguity
d. writers	d. holystic	d. is	d. indiligent	d. principle

Each of the following five questions (36-40) contains a brief passage which describes a regulation, procedure or law, followed by a situation. Read both, then answer the question(s) following each passage by applying the regulation, procedure, or law contained in the passage.

36. **Fire Emergency Procedure:**
"In this complex premises, the emergency arrangements are designed to allow people who are not at immediate risk from a fire to delay starting their evacuation. It may be appropriate to start the evacuation by initially evacuating only the area closest to the fire and warning other people to stand by. This is normally done by immediately evacuating the floor where the fire is located and the floor above. The other floors are then evacuated one by one to avoid congestion on the escape routes. The rest of the people are then evacuated if it is necessary to do so...In hospitals and care homes the floor may be divided into a number of fire resisting compartments and the occupants are moved from the compartment involved in fire to the adjacent compartment and if necessary moved again. Depending on the fire situation, it may eventually be necessary to consider vertical evacuation."(5)

Situation:
Court Officer-Trainee Gloria Delmar is patrolling the seventh floor hall when she discovers smoke coming out of one of the empty courtrooms on that floor. She immediately radios the Court Officer Headquarters in the building, informs them of the emergency situation, and then waits for appropriate personnel to arrive.

36. Based on the above procedure and situation, which of the following is the first and best action that Court Officer Delmar should take while she waits for appropriate personnel to arrive?
A. Immediately question nearby individuals to ascertain who might have started the fire.
B. Run into the room and try to extinguish the fire with a fire extinguisher that is mounted on the wall of the hall.
C. Instruct all nearby persons to evacuate the floor.
D. Tap into the building public announcements system and announce an emergency evacuation of the building.

Answer questions 37 and 38 based on the following section of Criminal Procedure Law and the situation described:

37.**Criminal Procedure Law (CPL) 160.10:**
Fingerprinting; duties of police with respect thereto
(For purposes of this exam, this section also applies to Court Officers)
1. Following an arrest, or following the arraignment upon a local criminal court accusatory instrument of a defendant whose court attendance has been secured by a summons or an appearance ticket under circumstances described in sections 130.60 and 150.70, the arresting or other appropriate police officer or agency must take or cause to be taken fingerprints of the arrested person or defendant if an offense which is the subject of the arrest or which is charged in the accusatory instrument filed is:
  (a) A felony; or
  (b) A misdemeanor defined in the penal law; or

(c) A misdemeanor defined outside the penal law which would constitute a felony if such person had a previous judgment of conviction for a crime; or

(d) Loitering for the purpose of engaging in a prostitution offense as defined in subdivision two of section 240.37 of the penal law.

2. In addition, a police officer who makes an arrest for any offense, either with or without a warrant, may take or cause to be taken the fingerprints of the arrested person if such police officer:

(a) Is unable to ascertain such person's identity; or

(b) Reasonably suspects that the identification given by such person is not accurate; or

(c) Reasonably suspects that such person is being sought by law enforcement officials for the commission of some other offense."

Situation: Court Officer Natalie Morrison arrests a male named Martin Hayle. Her authority to arrest Martin Hayle was a warrant issued by the court. The criminal offense stated in the warrant was the misdemeanor offense of "Obstructing Firefighting Operations (Penal Law 195.15). At the same time that she arrested Martin Hayle, his companion resisted the arrest by interposing her body between Court Officer Morrison and Martin Hayle. Because of this, Court Officer Morrison arrested the female for the misdemeanor offense of "Obstructing Governmental Operations." (Penal Law 195.05).

37. Based on the above Procedure (Law) and Situation, which of the following is Court Officer Morrison authorized to do?

A. Court Officer Natalie Morrison may fingerprint the person whom she alleges obstructed governmental administration because she has such authority under Criminal Procedure Law 160.10 Section 1 (d).

B. Court Officer Natalie Morrison may fingerprint only one of the two individuals she arrested because she does not have authority to fingerprint the second person.

C. Court Officer Natalie Morrison is authorized to fingerprint both persons under CPL 160.10.

D. Because of CPL 160.10, Court Officer Morrison may fingerprint one of the persons because she is mandated to do so, and may, at her discretion, fingerprint the second person.

•

38. Based on the above Procedure (Law) and Situation, which of the following statements is most correct?

A. If the arrested person is not charged with a felony, he may never be fingerprinted.

B. If a police officer believes an arrested person is giving false ID, that person must be fingerprinted.

C. Loitering for prostitution is defined in the Criminal Procedure Law.

D. If a police officer reasonably suspects that the identification given by such person is not accurate, he may take fingerprints.

•

Answer questions 39 and 40 based on the following "Fees for Nonpayment and Holdover cases" and the situation described.

39. **Procedure:** The "Fees for Nonpayment and Holdover cases "(both in Landlord and Tenant Court) are as follows: The minimum fee for the initiation of a Nonpayment case is $30.00, and for a Holdover case the minimum fee is $40.00. Because of the recent amendment to Article 80 of the CPLR, a surcharge is to be added to each case that is initiated: $2.50 for each Nonpayment case and $3.25 for each Holdover case initiated. In addition, the fee, starting July 21, 2019, for every Nonpayment and Holdover case initiated must include a $6.75 fee for postage expense.

Situation:

On July 21, 2019, Court Officer Wilma Chin is filling-in for a few minutes for a clerk at the Landlord and Tenant intake counter. An attorney brings in two Landlord and Tenant cases to be initiated (One

Nonpayment case and two Holdover cases). He also brings in a check for $132.25 to cover all initiation fees for the three cases.

39. Based on the preceding procedure and situation, which of the following statements regarding the processing of the cases by Court Officer Wilma Chin is most correct?
A. Court Officer Wilma Chin should initiate the three cases and collect the fee of $132.25, which is the same amount as the check.
B. The $6.75 fee may be waived because the increase takes effect on July 22, 2019.
C. The correct total amount the Court Officer Chin should collect is $125.50.
D. Court Officer Chin should inform the attorney that the fees for the three cases is $6.75 more than the
   check amount.

•

40. **Situation:**
Sam Tasmin, a landlord, wishes to initiate a Landlord and Tenant Nonpayment case. He hands Court Officer Chin the required papers and a check for $32.25. He states that he is not paying the postage fee because he wishes to deliver the papers to the tenant himself.

40. Based on the preceding procedure and situation, which of the following statements regarding the processing of the cases by Court Officer Wilma Chin is most correct?
A. Court Officer Chin should process the papers, collect the $32.25 fee, and permit Mr. Tasmin to deliver the papers himself.
B. Court Officer Chin should inform Mr. Tasmin that the correct fee is $50.00.
C. Court Officer Chin should inform Mr. Tasmin that the correct fee is $39.00 and that the court will deliver the papers by mail.
D. Court Officer Chin should inform Mr. Tasmin that he should hire a lawyer since he does not understand the case initiation procedures.

•

Remembering Facts and Information (Questions 41 - 55)

Directions:

When instructed by the test monitor, turn this page over and for the next 5 minutes, read the passage on the page as many times as you want. Try to memorize as many details of the passage as you can. At the end of the 5 minutes, when the test monitor instructs you to do so, stop reading and turn the page over. The test monitor will then collect this page.

(After the next 10 minutes, the test monitor will distribute the test booklets. When instructed to do so by the test monitor, open the test booklet and answer the first 15 questions in the booklet.)

On January 21, 2019, seven inches of snow had already covered the sidewalks by 8:30 a.m. Court Officer Helen Jennings, who lived only six blocks from the criminal court building in downtown Brooklyn, received a phone call from her Lieutenant, James Cordan, who was confirming that she would be coming to work, since more than half of the Court Officers in the command had already called that they would be unable to make the commute to work. Officer Jennings told her Lieutenant that she was just about to leave her house and that she would arrive at the court house before 9 a.m. On the way to the courthouse, Court Officer Jennings purchased a coffee and a bagel at City Donut, one block away from the criminal court building. When she arrived at the building at 279 Worthman Street, she noticed that two of the four magnetometers situated at the entrance of the building were not in operation and that each of the other two active magnetometers had only one Court Officer attending to it. The two Court Officers gave her a warm greeting. Court Officer Lance Thomas told her that so far only twelve Court Officers (including Court Officer Jennings) had arrived and that only three of the twenty-two judges had made it in. Court Officer Theresa Ming said that Major Kensington called that he was about twenty blocks away and that he would be arriving at about 9:30 a.m.

Court Officer Jennings quickly got into her uniform and reported to Lieutenant Cordan at 8:58 a.m. For most of the morning, Court Officer Jennings by herself did security patrol on floors 2, 3, and 4, something that was usually done by three Court Officers. Fortunately, only three of the fifteen parts were open on those floors, and the number of people was only about twenty percent of normal volume. Court Officer Jennings worked through lunch and then worked in Trial Part 26 in the afternoon. The Judge in the Part 26, Judge Manuel Thompson, thanked her for coming to work, as did Major Kensington during his afternoon rounds of the building. Most of the Court Officers who had long commutes left at 5:00 p.m. However, because Court Officer Jennings lived nearby, she volunteered for the 5:00 p.m. - 6:00 p.m. security detail. Although the snow was still coming down when she left at 6:15 p.m., she arrived home at 6:40 p.m.

•

41. The address of the Criminal Court building is:
    A. 259 Workman Street
    B. 295 Workmen Street
    C. 297 Worthmen Street
    D. 279 Worthman Street

42. The last name of the Major referred to in the passage is:
    A. Cordan
    B. Ming
    C. Kensington
    D. Thompson

43. Court Officer Jennings bought a coffee and bagel at:
    A. NYC Donut Shop
    B. City Donut
    C. City Donuts and Bagels
    D. NYC Coffee Shop

44. How many magnetometers were located at the entrance of the criminal court building?
    A. three
    B. two
    C. four
    D. none of the above

45. Most of the Court Officers who had long commutes left at:
    A. 5:00 p.m.
    B. 5:30 p.m.
    C. 6:00 p.m.
    D. 6:15 p.m.

46. The passage describes incidents that happened on what date?
    A. January 21, 2018
    B. January 21, 2019
    C. January 12, 2018
    D. January 12, 2019

47. In what number part did Court Officer Jennings work in the afternoon?
    A. Part 9
    B. Part 29
    C. Part 26
    D. Part 6

48. The volume of people in the afternoon was _____ percent of the usual volume.
    A. ten percent
    B. twenty percent
    C. thirty percent
    D. forty percent

49. How many inches of snow had covered the sidewalk by 8:30 a.m.?
    A. three
    B. four
    C. six
    D. seven

50. Which Court Officer said that Major Kensington called that he was about twenty blocks away?
    A. Court Officer Cordan
    B. Court Officer Theresa Ming
    C. Court Officer Thomas
    D. Court Officer Madison

51. Court Officer Jennings arrived at home at:
    A. 5:40 p.m.
    B. 6:00 p.m.
    C. 6:40 p.m.
    D. 6:00 a.m.

52. The last name of the judge in Part 26 was:
    A. Thomas
    B. Thompson
    C. Kensington
    D. Cordan

53. What did Court Officer Jennings purchase on her way to work?
    A. Tea and donut
    B. Coffee and bagel
    C. Coffee and jelly donut
    D. Coffee and muffin

54. How far away from the coffee shop was the court building?
    A. three blocks
    B one block
    C. two blocks
    D. none of the above

55. What was the number of total Parts open on floors 2, 3 and 4?
    A. 3
    B. seven
    C. 15
    D. none of the above

Questions 56-70

Directions:
The following 15 questions are based on the following three tables (Daily Log of Cases - Civil Court; Daily Log of Cases - Criminal Court; Daily Log of Cases - Family Court). First, fill-in the two cells with the notations "1?" and "2?", then answer the 15 questions based on the information in the three tables. Two supplementary tables, "Daily Breakdown of Cases (Civil Court, Criminal Court and Family Court"; and "Summary of Cases (Civil Court, Criminal Court and Family Court)" are provided to help you organize the information so that you will be able to answer the questions correctly. Only the answers will be graded.

The following is a log of cases in Civil Court Conference Parts on September 12, 2019. Cases are conferenced in these Parts and they are either "Adjourned", "Dismissed" or "Settled" (settled with a money award, or settled-with no money award).

Daily Log of Cases - September 12, 2019 Civil Court			
Judge	**Date Filed**	**Status**	**Money Award**
Rampor	06/12/17	Settled	X
Thompson	04/08/18	Dismissed	X
Wang	01/05/19	(1?)	$15,400
Thompson	06/25/18	Settled	X
Thompson	09/22/18	Adjourned	X
Rampor	08/17/18	Dismissed	X
Wang	09/21/17	Adjourned	X
Rampor	11/15/18	Adjourned	X
Thompson	11/15/17	Settled	$13,500
Rampor	07/19/18	Adjourned	X
Wang	02/16/19	Dismissed	X
Thompson	09/27/17	Settled	$17,200
Wang	06/10/18	Settled	$24,500
Rampor	05/13/17	Adjourned	X
Thompson	02/09/18	Settled	$22,900

The following is a log of cases of Criminal Court Cases on September 12, 2019. Cases appeared in front of the following judges and were "Adjourned", "Dismissed", or "Disposed" (with either a jail "Sentence" or with "No sentence").

	Daily Log of Cases - September 12, 2019 Criminal Court		
Judge	Date Filed	Status	Sentence
Wilks	05/13/18	(2?)	Sentence
Rodriguez	03/07/19	Adjourned	X
Cohen	02/04/19	Adjourned	X
Rodriguez	05/24/19	Disposed	No Sentence
Rodriguez	08/21/18	Adjourned	X
Wilks	07/18/19	Dismissed	X
Cohen	08/20/17	Adjourned	X
Wilks	04/14/19	Disposed	Sentence
Rodriguez	06/16/18	Dismissed	X
Wilks	05/18/18	Disposed	Sentence
Cohen	04/15/19	Adjourned	X
Rodriguez	07/26/19	Disposed	No sentence
Cohen	05/11/17	Disposed	Sentence
Wilks	04/12/18	Dismissed	X
Cohen	02/09/19	Adjourned	X

On the following pages, there are tables for "Daily Log of Cases Logs of Family Court" for September 12, 2019 and blank "Summary of Cases September 12, 2019" (Civil, Criminal and Family Courts).

Cases in Family Court that were not "Adjourned" or "Dismissed" were "Disposed" (either through "Hearing Complete" or "PINS Referral").

Daily Log of Cases - September 12, 2019
Family Court

Judge	Date Filed	Status	Completion
Baker	02/11/17	Dismissed	X
Visilov	02/05/19	Adjourned	X
Ruggiero	01/07/18	Disposed	PINS Referral
Ruggiero	03/21/19	Adjourned	X
Baker	06/19/18	Dismissed	X
Visilov	02/12/19	Disposed	PINS Referral
Baker	06/22/18	Disposed	Hearing Complete
Ruggiero	03/09/19	Dismissed	X
Visilov	04/15/18	Adjourned	X
Ruggiero	06/19/19	Disposed	Hearing Complete
Visilov	02/13/19	Adjourned	X
Baker	05/12/17	Disposed	Hearing Complete
Baker	07/16/19	Dismissed	X
Visilov	03/13/18	Disposed	PINS Referral
Baker	06/11/19	Disposed	PINS Referral

Summary of Cases September 12, 2019
(Civil, Criminal and Family Courts)

Status of Case	Civil	Criminal	Family	Cases Total
Adjourned				
Dismissed				
Disposed - Sentence				
Disposed - No Sentence				
Disposed - Hearing Complete				
Disposed - PINS Referral				
Settled - No money Award				
Settled - Money Award				
Total Cases				
Cases Filed by Year				
2017				
2018				
2019				
Total Cases				

Judge	Dismissed	Adjourned	Settled With No Money Award	Settled With Money Award	Disposed With PINS Referral	Disposed Hearing Complete	Disposed With Sentence	Disposed With No Sentence	Total Cases
Summary of Cases (Civil, Criminal, Family)									
Rampor									
Thompson									
Wang									
Wilks									
Rodriguez									
Cohen									
Baker									
Visilov									
Ruggiero									

56. The total number of criminal court adjourned cases exceeded the total number of family court adjourned cases by:
   A. 1
   B. 2
   C. 3
   D. none of the above

57. The total number of 2019 cases for Civil, Criminal, and Family Court is:
   A. 9
   B. 16
   C. 17
   D. 18

58. How many cases were "Settled - Money Award"?
   A. 3
   B. 4
   C. 5
   D. 6

59. How many cases did Judge Thompson "Settle With Money Award"?
   A. 1
   B. 2
   C. 3
   D. none of the above

60. The total number of cases handled by Judges Baker and Visilov is:
   A. 10
   B. 11
   C. 12
   D. none of the above

61. Which two Judges tied for handling the greatest number of cases?
    A. Judge Wang and Judge Rampor
    B. Judge Rampor and Judge Rodriguez
    C. Judge Rodriguez and Judge Baker
    D. Judge Thompson and Judge Baker

62. What is the total number of adjourned cases for all 3 courts combined?
    A. 14
    B. 15
    C. 16
    D. none of the above

63. Which two Judges tied for the least number of cases handled?
    A. Judge Wang and Judge Ruggiero
    B. Judge Visilov and Judge Cohen
    C. Judge Rampor and Judge Rodriguez
    D. Judge Wilks and Jude Ruggiero

64. What is the total number of cases for Civil Court plus Criminal Court?
    A. 15
    B. 30
    C. 45
    D. 60

65. How many cases were "Disposed With PINS Referral"?
    A. 2
    B. 3
    C. 4
    D. none of the above

66. What is the total number of cases handled by all three courts?
    A. 15
    B. 40
    C. 65
    D. none of the above

67. Which court dismissed the greatest number of cases?
    A. Family court
    B. Criminal court
    C. Family court
    D. none of the above. All three courts dismissed an equal number of cases.

68. The total number of 2018 cases handled by all courts exceeded the total number of 2017 cases by:
    A. 9
    B. 18
    C. 26
    D. 8

69. How many Family court cases were "Disposed - PINS Referral"?
    A. 2
    B. 3
    C. 4
    D. 5

70. What is the total of 2017 cases and 2018 cases?
    A. 36
    B. 18
    C. 9
    D. 27

PRACTICE TEST
ANSWERS

Clerical Checking

Instructions: Questions 1-10 (below) consist of three sets of information. Compare the information in each set and mark your answer sheet, as follows:

Mark: Choice A if all three sets are exactly alike
         Choice B if none of the three sets are exactly alike.
         Choice C if only the second and third sets are exactly alike
         Choice D if only the first and second sets are exactly alike

---

1. 897454-237852 KCV-26
Rooms 8132, 4859, 6031
SCPA 4052 and CPL 4491
5/18/18, 7/13/20, 8/1/21
8743 Farmers Drive, (NY)

1. 897454-237852 KCV-26
Rooms 8132, 4859, 6031
SCPA 4052 and CPL 4491
5/18/18, 7/13/20, 8/1/21
8743 Farmers Drive, (NY)

1. 897454-237852 KCV-26
Rooms 8132, 4859, 6031
SCPA 4052 and CPL 4491 **A**
5/18/18, 7/13/20, 8/1/21
8743 Farmers Drive, (NY)

2. Sgt. John Boulderman, Jr.
Court Int. Grace Kravitz
Witness: Nancy Ann Ecker
Summary Rep. 6912: 5 Folio
G: 4857834-292 (Series L-B)

2. Sgt. John Boulderman, Jr.
Court Int. Grace Kra**vits**
Witness: Nancy Ann Ecker
Summary Rep. 6912: 5 Folio
G: 4857834-292 (Series L-B)

2. Sgt. John Boulder**men**, Jr.
Court Int. Grace Kravitz
Witness: Nancy Ann Ecker **B**
Summary Rep. 6912: 5 Folio
G: 4857834-292 (Series L-B)

3. Social Services DK-21949
Court Reporter Samsoned
Judge Richard Wescott Sr.
Priority (MS-2-5893439354)
Gugenheim and Bakersville

3. Social Services DK-21949
Court Reporter Samsoned
Judge Richard Wescott Sr.
Priority (MS-2-5893439354)
Gugenheim and Bakersville

3. Social Services DK-21949
Court Reporter Samsoned
Judge Richard Wescott Sr.
Priority (MS-2-5893439**854**) **D**
Gugenheim and Bakersville

4. MOH: 4/21/19, 11/25/19
Kings, NY 11275-2267
Seq. Ref.: Q-317-51362
Leiman Bri**skol** (Oswego)
557 Bay Parkway, 2nd floor

4. MOH: 4/21/19, 11/25/19
Kings, NY 11275-2267
Seq. Ref.: Q-317-51362
Leiman Briskoll (Oswego)
557 Bay Parkway, 2nd floor

4. MOH: 4/21/19, 11/25/19
Kings, NY 11275-2267
Seq. Ref.: Q-317-51362   **C**
Leiman Briskoll (Oswego)
557 Bay Parkway, 2nd floor

5. FCA Section **3028(c)** (2018)
Court Assistant Overman
ID # 4649517566-750-2018
221800-B Vanders Highway
Leonard Harrison, ID: H-3238

5. FCA Section 3028(e) (2018)
Court Assistant Overman
ID # 4649517566-750-2018
221800-B **Vander** Highway
Leonard Harrison, ID: H-3238

5. FCA Section 3028(e) (2018)
Court Assistant Overman
ID # 4649517566-750-2018 **B**
221800-B Vanders Highway
Leonard Harrison, ID: H-3238

6. 225 S. Beachgate, NJ
Evidence and Records Dept.
Judge David M. Faulkner
Req. #:2547/2018 (Neiman)
Sealed file R:38972/2019

6. 225 S. Beachgate, NJ
Evidence and Records Dept.
Judge David M. Faulkner
Req. #:2547/2018 (Neiman)
Sealed file R:38972/2019

6. 225 S. Beachgate, NJ
Evidence and Records Dept.
Judge David M. Faulkner **D**
Req. #:2547/2018 (**Nieman**)
Sealed file R:38972/2019

7. Kermini, Samuel (Family Ct.)
   (267) 432-1548 (8 a.m.)
   Outerbanks, NJ, 20236
   142-50 S. Jersey Highway
   Examiner Lyndon Rockerfeller

8. Happy **Vally**, NY 12739-2428
   Nervana Circle 12683-9758
   Justice Luke Wortman-Ellis
   ID: 263214853-73599326
   Reg. 3059/D-254 (e) and (g)

9. Harmon, Spelling, & Jones
   Civil Court Pub. 2019-12P
   1832 Marmon St., Suite 5
   New York, NY 10032-2366
   ID #: 486452-2018 (F)

10. Brooklyn, NY **11229**-6017
    CR Benjamin F. Bowman
    2743-02-5208 and 872-36
    Rooms (502), (5498), (9781)
    SCPA 2019 (Section 1065)

7. Kermini, Samuel (Family Ct.)
   (267) 432-1548 (8 a.m.)
   Outerbanks, NJ, 20236
   142-50 S. Jersey Highway
   Examiner Lyndon Rockerfeller

8. Happy Valley, NY 12739-2428
   Nervana Circle 12683-9758
   Justice Luke Wortman-Ellis
   ID: 263214853-73599326
   Reg. 3059/D-254 (e) and (g)

9. Harmon, Spelling, & Jones
   Civil Court Pub. 2019-12P
   1832 Marmon St., Suite 5
   New York, NY 10032-2366
   ID #: 486452-2018 (F)

10. Brooklyn, NY 11259-6017
    CR Benjamin F. Bow**men**
    2743-02-5208 and 872-36
    Rooms (502), (5498), (9781)
    SCPA 2019 (Section 1065)

7. Kermini, Samuel (Family Ct.)
   (267) 432-1548 (8 a.m.)
   Outerbanks, NJ, 20236   **D**
   142-50 S. Jersey Highway
   Examiner Lyndon **Rockefeller**

8. Happy Valley, NY 12739-2428
   Nervana Circle 12683-9758
   Justice Luke Wortman-Ellis **C**
   ID: 263214853-73599326
   Reg. 3059/D-254 (e) and (g)

9. Harmon, Spelling, & Jones
   Civil Court Pub. 2019-12P
   1832 Marmon St., Suite 5   **A**
   New York, NY 10032-2366
   ID #: 486452-2018 (F)

10. Brooklyn, NY 11259-6017
    CR Benjamin F. Bowman
    2743-02-5208 and 872-36 **B**
    Rooms (502), (5498), (9781)
    SCPA 2019 (Section 1065)

Instructions; Questions 11-20 (below) consist of three sets of information. Compare the information in each set and mark your answer sheet, as follows:
A. Only the second and third sets are exactly alike
B. Only the first and second sets are exactly alike
C. None of the sets are exactly alike
D. All three sets are exactly alike

11. 42565933922-4806
    Specter Street, NJ
    James Albert Wayings
    Assault, second degree
    Kevin F. Bromowitz

12. 427354-348967 COS3-2
    Suites 5625, 3855, 7035
    CPLR 1102 and CPL 44427
    4/21/18, 6/12/19, 12/3/19
    57472 Taylor Circle, (NJ)

13. Sgt. Gill Borman, Jr.
    Sayville: J. Edmont, Sn.
    George V. Mantions, Jr.
    CV Numb. 3957: (3865348)
    N: 1693952-2528 (Ser. K-N)

11. 42565933922-4806
    Specter Street, NJ
    James Albert Wayings
    Assault, second degree
    Kevin F. Bromowitz

12. 427354-348967 COS3-2
    Suites 5625, 3855, 7035
    CPLR 1102 and CPL 44427
    4/21/18, 6/12/19, 12/3/19
    57472 Taylor Circle, (NJ)

13. Sgt. Gill Borman, Jr.
    Sayville: J. Edmont, Sn.
    George V. Mantions, Jr.
    CV Numb. 3957: (3865348)
    N: 1693952-**2928** (Ser. K-N)

11. 42565933**952**-4806
    Specter Street, NJ
    James Albert Wayings **B**
    Assault, second degree
    Kevin F. Bromowitz

12. 427354-348967 COS3-2
    Suites 5625, 3855, 7035
    CPLR 1102 and CPL **4427 B**
    4/21/18, 6/12/19, 12/3/19
    57472 Taylor Circle, (NJ)

13. Sgt. **Jill** Borman, Jr.
    Sayville: J. Edmont, Sn.
    George V. Mantions, Jr.   **C**
    CV Numb. 3957: (3865348)
    N: 1693952-2528 (Ser. K-N)

Court Officer New York State (NYS Court Officer-Trainee)

14. Inc. Report SSN 2809237
Junior Clerk L. Simons
CO - Lawrence Washington
Vol. (SDK-2 - 3869764-4392)
Cloverfield and Lawtonfille 3

15. Beacon, NY 11508-2673
JHO Nancy Heath**erfeld**
422-37-7243 and 4285-58
Rooms (404-A), (659 -CB)
Appellate Division, 2 Dept.

16. Wernor Junction, NJ 07039
Seaton Lane (West 315657)
Judge Saverio Appertino
ID: 386842254-75239656
Reg. 6039/D-853 (xw) and (d)

17. Furlow, Brandenstin, Rogers
Criminal Procedure Law
73-49 Hea**thurs** Boulevard
Yonkers, NY 10732-3295
Ref. #: 6895252-1579 (B-D)

18. 30953392-398494 SAR-525
Supply Rms. 369, 8825, 7037
EPT 301(c) & CPL 6224(d)
9/2/18, 9/9/19, 5/8/19, 6/7/19
7742 Darwin Avenue, (CT)

19. Sgt. Solomon Beckers-Chin
Ct. Off. Sgt. Maria Latnova
Ct. Rep. Mohamed Ayman
UIR 799735: 9 Series K-M
G: 9697974-336 (Series E-P)

20. Daily W-234468148**959**
Ct. Officer J. Lumowitz, Sr.
Magistrate M. J. Ermigton
Seq. (ABDS 2 - 487023841)
Mohamed Alvarez: 3735822

---

14. Inc. Report SSN 2809237
Junior Clerk L. Simons
CO - Lawrence Washington
Vol. (SDK-2 - 3869764-4392)
Cloverfield and Lawtonfille 3

15. Beacon, NY 11508-2673
JHO Nancy Heatherfield
422-37-7243 and 4285-58
Rooms (404-A), (659 -CB)
Appellate Division, 2 Dept.

16. Wernor Junction, **NY** 07039
Seaton Lane (West 315657)
Judge Saverio Appertino
ID: 386842254-75239656
Reg. 6039/D-853 (xw) and (d)

17. Furlow, Brandenstin, Rogers
Criminal Procedure Law
73-49 Heathers Boulevard
Yonkers, NY 10732-3295
Ref. #: 6895252-1579 (B-D)

18. 30953392-398494 SAR-525
Supply Rms. 369, 8825, 7037
EPT 301(c) & CPL 6224(d)
9/2/18, 9/9/19, 5/8/19, 6/7/19
7742 Darwin Avenue, (CT)

19. Sgt. Solomon Beckers-Chin
Ct. Off. Sgt. Maria Latnova
Ct. Rep. Mohamed Ayman
UIR 799735: 9 Series K-M
G: 9697974-336 (Series E-P)

20. Daily W-234468148929
Ct. Officer J. Lum**owits,** Sr.
Magistrate M. J. Ermigton
Seq. (ABDS 2 - 487023841)
Mohamed Alvarez: 3735822

---

14. Inc. Report SSN 2809237
Junior Clerk L. Simons
CO - Lawrence Washington **D**
Vol. (SDK-2 - 3869764-4392)
Cloverfield and Lawtonfille 3

15. Beacon, NY 11508-2673
JHO Nancy Heatherfield
422-37-7243 and 4285-58 **A**
Rooms (404-A), (659 -CB)
Appellate Division, 2 Dept.

16. Wernor Junction, NJ 07039
Seaton Lane (West 315657)
Judge Saverio Appertino **C**
ID: 386842254-75239656
Reg. 6039/D-853 **(xy)** and (d)

17. Furlow, Brandenstin, Rogers
Criminal Procedure Law
73-49 Heathers Boulevard **A**
Yonkers, NY 10732-3295
Ref. #: 6895252-1579 (B-D)

18. 30953392-398494 SAR-525
Supply Rms. 369, 8825, 7037
EPT 301(c) & CPL 6224(d) **B**
9/28, 9/9/19, 5/8/19, **6/7/15**
7742 Darwin Avenue, (CT)

19. Sgt. Solomon Beckers-Chin
Ct. Off. Sgt. Maria Latnova
Ct. Rep. Mohamed Ayman **D**
UIR 799735: 9 Series K-M
G: 9697974-336 (Series E-P)

20. Daily W-234468148929
Ct. Officer J. Lumowitz, Sr.
Magistrate M. J. Ermigton **C**
Seq. (ABDS 2 - 487023841)
Mohamed Alvarez: 3735822

Reading and Understanding Written Material
Format A: Understanding the content of a written passage

For the following questions (21-25) read the passage and then answer the question based solely on the information provided in the passage.

21. "Smoking bans are enacted in an attempt to protect people from the effects of second-hand smoke, which include an increased risk of heart disease, cancer, emphysema, and other diseases. Laws implementing bans on indoor smoking have been introduced by many countries in various forms over the years, with some legislators citing scientific evidence that shows tobacco smoking is harmful to the smokers themselves and to those inhaling second-hand smoke. In addition such laws may reduce health care costs, improve work productivity, and lower the overall cost of labor in the community thus protected, making that workforce more attractive for employers. In the US state of Indiana, the economic development agency included in its 2006 plan for acceleration of economic growth encouragement for cities and towns to adopt local smoking bans as a means of promoting job growth in communities."(4)

21. According to the above passage:
A. Illinois is a U.S. state.
   WRONG: The passage does not mention Illinois. <u>Indiana</u> is a US state.
B. Laws implementing bans on outdoor smoking have been introduced by many countries.
   WRONG: Laws implementing bans on <u>indoor</u> smoking have been introduced by many countries.
C. The US government economic development agency included in its 2006 plan for acceleration of economic growth encouragement for promoting job growth.
   WRONG: <u>The US state of Indiana</u> economic development agency included in its 2006 plan for acceleration of economic growth encouragement for promoting job growth.
D. An effect of second-hand smoke is increased risk of emphysema.
   CORRECT ANSWER

22. "Many in the United States use the word bailiff colloquially to refer to a peace officer providing court security. More often, these Court Officers are sheriff's deputies, marshals, corrections officers or constables. The terminology varies among (and sometimes within) the several states. In rural areas, this responsibility is often carried out by the junior lawyer in training under the judge's supervision called a law clerk who also has the title of bailiff. Whatever the name used, the agency providing court security is often charged with serving legal process and seizing and selling property (e.g., replevin or foreclosure). In some cases, the duties are separated between agencies in a given jurisdiction. For instance, a Court Officer may provide courtroom security in a jurisdiction where a sheriff or constable handles service of process and seizures....In the New York State Unified Court System, Court Officers, are responsible for providing security and enforcing the law in and around court houses. Under New York State penal code, they are classified as "peace officers." New York State Court Officers are able to carry firearms both on and off duty, and have the power to make warrantless arrests both on and off duty anywhere in the State of New York. They also have the authority to make traffic stops."(4)

22. According to the above passage, which of the following four choices is correct?
A. In New York State, Court Officers are police officers.
   WRONG: In New York State, Court Officers are <u>peace</u> officers.
B. A New York State Court Officer may make arrests in any part of New York State.
   CORRECT. "New York State Court Officers...have the power to make warrantless arrests...anywhere in the State of New York."
C. NYS Court Officers may only carry a gun while on duty.
   WRONG: "New York State Court Officers are able to carry firearms both on and off duty."

D. Court Officers do not have authority to make traffic stops.
  WRONG: " They also have the authority to make traffic stops."

———

23."Preponderance of the evidence, also known as balance of probabilities, is the standard required in most civil cases and in family court determinations solely involving money, such as child support under the Child Support Standards Act. It is also the burden of proof of which the defendant must prove affirmative defenses or mitigating circumstances in civil or criminal court. In civil court, aggravating circumstances also only have to be proven by a preponderance of the evidence, as opposed to beyond reasonable doubt (as they do in criminal court). The standard is met if the proposition is more likely to be true than not true. The standard is satisfied if there is greater than fifty percent chance that the proposition is true. Lord Denning, in Miller v. Minister of Pensions, described it simply as "more probable than not." Until 1970, this was also the standard used in juvenile court in the United States. This is also the standard of proof used when determining eligibility of unemployment benefits for a former employee accused of losing the job through alleged misconduct. In most US states, the employer must prove this case with a preponderance of evidence. Preponderance of the evidence is the standard of proof used for immunity from prosecution under Florida's controversial stand-your-ground law. The defense must present its evidence in a pre-trial hearing, show that the statutory prerequisites have been met, and then request that the court grant a motion for declaration of immunity. The judge must then decide from the preponderance of the evidence whether to grant immunity. This is a far lower burden than "beyond a reasonable doubt," the threshold a prosecutor must meet at any proceeding criminal trial, but higher than the "probable cause" threshold generally required for indictment."(4)

23 Based on the above passage, which of the following four statements is not correct?
A. **"Beyond a reasonable doubt," is a lower burden than "preponderance of the evidence."**
  THIS IS THE ANSWER. Preponderance of the evidence" is a far lower burden than "beyond a reasonable doubt,"
B. "Preponderance of the evidence" is the standard of proof used for immunity from prosecution under Florida's controversial stand-your-ground law.
  This statement is correct. The passage clearly states this.
C. "Preponderance of the evidence" is satisfied if there is greater than fifty percent chance that the proposition is true.
  This statement is correct. The passage clearly states this.
D. "Preponderance of the evidence" standard is the required standard in most civil cases and in family court determinations solely involving money.
  This statement is correct. The passage clearly states this.

•

24. "A defined benefit pension plan is a type of pension plan in which an employer/sponsor promises a specified pension payment, lump-sum (or combination thereof) on retirement that is predetermined by a formula based on the employee's earnings history, tenure of service and age, rather than depending directly on individual investment returns. Traditionally, many governmental and public entities, as well as a large number of corporations, provided defined benefit plans, sometimes as a means of compensating workers in lieu of increased pay. A defined benefit plan is 'defined' in the sense that the benefit formula is defined and known in advance. Conversely, for a "defined contribution retirement saving plan", the formula for computing the employer's and employee's contributions is defined and known in advance, but the benefit to be paid out is not known in advance...When participating in a defined benefit pension plan, an employer/sponsor promises to pay the employees/members a specific benefit for life beginning at retirement. The benefit is calculated in advance using a formula based on age, earnings, and years of service. In the United States, the maximum retirement benefit permitted in 2014 under a defined benefit plan is $210,000 (up from $205,000 in 2013). Defined benefit pension plans in the U.S. currently do not have contribution limits."(4)

24. According to the above passage, which of the following four statements is not correct?
A. Defined benefit pension plans in the U.S. currently do not have contribution limits.
B. In a defined benefit plan, the benefit formula is known in advance.
C. **An employer/sponsor promises to pay the employees/members a specific benefit for life beginning at the age of 62.**
   THIS IS THE ANSWER. "An employer/sponsor promises to pay the employees/members a specific benefit for life beginning at <u>retirement</u>" (and not necessarily at age 62).
D. Many governmental entities provide defined benefit plans.

•

25. "Crowd control is a public security practice where large crowds are managed to prevent the outbreak of crowd crushes, affray, fights involving drunk and disorderly people or riots. Crowd crushes in particular can cause many hundreds of fatalities. Effective crowd management is about managing expected and unexpected crowd occurrences. Crowd control can involve privately hired security guards as well as police officers. Crowd control is often used at large, public gatherings like street fairs, music festivals, stadiums and public demonstrations. At some events, security guards and police use metal detectors and sniffer dogs to prevent weapons and drugs being brought into a venue....Materials such as stanchions, crowd control barriers, fences and decals painted on the ground can be used to direct a crowd. A common method of crowd control is to use high visibility fencing to divert and corral pedestrian traffic to safety when there is any potential threat for danger. Keeping the crowd comfortable and relaxed is also essential, so things like awnings, cooling fans (in hot weather), and entertainment are sometimes used as well."(4)

25. According to the above passage, which of the following four statements is not correct?
A. Preventing fights involving drunks is a part of crowd control.
B. Sniffer dogs are used to prevent weapons from being brought into a location.
C. **Because of the risk of violence, only police officers are used to effectively manage crowds.**
   THIS IS THE ANSWER. The passage states that BOTH <u>security guards and police officers</u> are used
      to manage crowds.
D. Cooling fans may be used to manage crowds.

•

Format B: Select the best alternative from four alternatives that best completes a sentence or passage.

Directions: (Questions 26 - 30) This section contains two passages. In each passage five words or phrases have been omitted. For each omitted word, select the one word or phrase from the four alternatives that best completes the passage.

Passage 1:
Court Officer-Trainees learn a great deal at the Court Officers Academy. However, they also learn many things thereafter. Much of this later learning comes from ___26___ received from their fellow Court Officers. One of the key suggestions offered by experienced officers is to constantly ___27___ good judgment instead of being ___28___ by rules which in many cases do not apply in every situation. For example, although a "No drinks allowed" sign may be posted on the wall, there may be cases where litigants (such as persons with diabetes) should be allowed to have a water bottle. ___29___
generally known that diabetics are ___30___ to dehydration and therefore must drink water as needed.

26. a. adviser	27. a. exorcise	28. a. indulged	29 a. His	30. a. suceptable
b. advize	b. exsercise	b. constrained	b. Its'	b. susceptible
c. advise	c. exercise	c. freed	c. Its	c. impervious
d. advice	d. excorcise	d. declined	d. It's	d. immune

Answers 1 - 5

26. **D** (correct spelling and meaning)
27. **C** (correct spelling and meaning)
28. **B** (vocabulary and logic; constrained means restricted in activity)
29. **D** (It's means "It is.")
30. **B** ("susceptible" means likely or liable to be harmed by something)

Passage 2:

"Diligent behavior is indicative of a work ethic; a belief that work is good in itself. Diligence is carefulness and persistent effort or work..." Some ___31___ suggest diligence in a student is defined as an effort he or she puts towards balanced and___32___ development in mental, physical, social and spiritual dimensions. They find diligence in students ___33___ correlated with academic performance. This is especially found in younger students. The support of parents and educators encourages students to be ___34___. Other factors which encourage diligence in students include motivation, discipline, concentration, responsibility and devotedness...Due diligence is the necessary amount of diligence required in a professional activity to avoid being negligent. This commonly arises in major acquisitions where the legal___35___ of caveat emptor ("let the buyer beware") requires the purchaser to make a diligent survey of the property or service being sold."(4)

31. a. body	32. a. hollistic	33. a. are	34. a. indigent	35. a. cavat
b. person	b. holistic	b. haven't	b. diligent	b. principal
c. individual	c. holistick	c. weren't	c. indilligent	c. ambiguity
d. writers	d. holystic	d. is	d. indiligent	d. principle

Answers 1 - 5

31. **D** (The plural verb "suggest" needs a plural subject, "writers".)
32. **B** (correct spelling)
33. **D** (The subject is singular "diligence in students", therefore verb must be singular "is".)
34. **B** (correct spelling and meaning)
35. **D** (correct spelling and meaning)

Each of the following five questions (36-40) contains a brief passage which describes a regulation, procedure or law, followed by a situation. Read both, then answer the question(s) following each passage by applying the regulation, procedure, or law contained in the passage.

36. **Fire Emergency Procedure:**
"In this complex premises, the emergency arrangements are designed to allow people who are not at immediate risk from a fire to delay starting their evacuation. It may be appropriate to start the evacuation by initially evacuating only the area closest to the fire and warning other people to stand by. This is normally done by immediately evacuating the floor where the fire is located and the floor above. The other floors are then evacuated one by one to avoid congestion on the escape routes. The rest of the people are then evacuated if it is necessary to do so...In hospitals and care homes the floor may be divided into a number of fire resisting compartments and the occupants are moved from the compartment involved in fire to the adjacent compartment and if necessary moved again. Depending on the fire situation, it may eventually be necessary to consider vertical evacuation."[5]

Situation:
Court Officer-Trainee Gloria Delmar is patrolling the seventh floor hall when she discovers smoke coming from an empty courtroom on that floor. She immediately radios the Court Officer Headquarters in the building, informs them of the emergency situation, and then waits for appropriate personnel to arrive.

36. Based on the above procedure and situation, which of the following is the first and best action that Court Officer Delmar should take while she waits for appropriate personnel to arrive?
A. Immediately question nearby individuals to ascertain who might have started the fire.
B. Run into the room and try to extinguish the fire with a fire extinguisher that is mounted on the wall of
    the hall.
C. Instruct all nearby persons to evacuate the floor.
D. Tap into the building public announcements system and announce an emergency evacuation of the building.

Choice "A" is not a good choice because there is a fire emergency which needs immediate attention. Any investigation can be done later.

Choice "B" is not the best choice because human life (in the hall) should be attended to first, as opposed to property.

Answer: Choice "C" is the best choice because it addresses the immediate danger.

Choice "D" is not a good choice because the extent of the emergency is not known yet and it is presumptuous and unauthorized for a Court Officer with limited facts to order the evacuation of the building.

Answer questions 37 and 38 based on the following section of Criminal Procedure Law and the situation described:

37. **Criminal Procedure Law (CPL) 160.10:**
Fingerprinting; duties of police with respect thereto
(For purposes of this exam, this section also applies to Court Officers)
1. Following an arrest, or following the arraignment upon a local criminal court accusatory instrument of a defendant whose court attendance has been secured by a summons or an appearance ticket under circumstances described in sections 130.60 and 150.70, the arresting or other appropriate

police officer or agency must take or cause to be taken fingerprints of the arrested person or defendant if an offense which is the subject of the arrest or which is charged in the accusatory instrument filed is:

(a) A felony; or

(b) A misdemeanor defined in the penal law; or

(c) A misdemeanor defined outside the penal law which would constitute a felony if such person had a previous judgment of conviction for a crime; or

(d) Loitering for the purpose of engaging in a prostitution offense as defined in subdivision two of section 240.37 of the penal law.

2. In addition, a police officer who makes an arrest for any offense, either with or without a warrant, may take or cause to be taken the fingerprints of the arrested person if such police officer:

(a) Is unable to ascertain such person's identity; or

(b) Reasonably suspects that the identification given by such person is not accurate; or

(c) Reasonably suspects that such person is being sought by law enforcement officials for the commission of some other offense."

Situation: Court Officer Natalie Morrison arrests a male named Martin Hayle. Her authority to arrest Martin Hayle was a warrant issued by the court. The criminal offense stated in the warrant was the misdemeanor offense of "Obstructing Firefighting Operations (Penal Law 195.15). At the same time that she arrested Martin Hayle, his companion resisted the arrest by interposing her body between Court Officer Morrison and Martin Hayle. Because of this, Court Officer Morrison arrested the female for the misdemeanor offense of "Obstructing Governmental Operations." (Penal Law 195.05).

37. Based on the above Procedure (Law) and Situation, which of the following is Court Officer Morrison authorized to do?

A. Court Officer Natalie Morrison may fingerprint the person whom she alleges obstructed governmental administration because she has such authority under Criminal Procedure Law 160.10 Section 1 (d).

B. Court Officer Natalie Morrison may fingerprint only one of the two individuals she arrested because she does not have authority to fingerprint the second person.

C. Court Officer Natalie Morrison is authorized to fingerprint both persons under CPL 160.10.

D. Because of CPL 160.10, Court Officer Morrison may fingerprint one of the persons because she is mandated to do so, and may, at her discretion, fingerprint the second person.

37. C Court Officer Natalie Morrison is authorized to fingerprint both persons under CPL 160.10. (Both offenses are misdemeanors defined in the Penal Law.)

Choice "A" is not correct because Criminal Procedure Law 160.10 Section 1 (d) deals with loitering for prostitution, which is not the reason the persons were arrested.

Choice "B" is not correct because both persons are accused of misdemeanors defined in the Penal Law and therefore must be fingerprinted.

Choice "D" is not correct because both persons are accused of misdemeanors defined in the Penal Law and therefore must be fingerprinted.

•

38. Based on the above Procedure (Law) and Situation, which of the following statements is most correct?

A. If the arrested person is not charged with a felony, he may never be fingerprinted.

B. If a police officer believes an arrested person is giving false ID, that person must be fingerprinted.

C. Loitering for prostitution is defined in the Criminal Procedure Law.

D. If a police officer reasonably suspects that the identification given by such person is not accurate, he may take fingerprints.

38. Choice "D" is the correct choice. D If a police officer reasonably suspects that the identification given by such person is not accurate, he may take fingerprints.
Choice "A" is not correct because the opposite is usually true.

Choice "B" is not correct because in that instance, the police officer MAY take fingerprints. The "MUST" in the sentence makes that choice not correct.

Choice "C" is not correct because loitering for prostitution is defined in the Penal Law and not the Criminal Procedure Law.

•

Answer questions 39 and 40 based on the following Procedure: "Fees for Nonpayment and Holdover cases" and the situation described.

39. Procedure: The "Fees for Nonpayment and Holdover cases "(both in Landlord and Tenant Court) are as follows: The minimum fee for the initiation of a Nonpayment case is $30.00, and for a Holdover case the minimum fee is $40.00. Because of the recent amendment to Article 80 of the CPLR, a surcharge is to be added to each case that is initiated: $2.50 for each Nonpayment case and $3.25 for each Holdover case initiated. In addition, the fee, starting July 21, 2019, for every Nonpayment and Holdover case initiated must include a $6.75 fee for postage expense.

Situation:
On July 21, 2019, Court Officer Wilma Chin is filling-in for a few minutes for a clerk at the Landlord and Tenant intake counter. An attorney brings in three Landlord and Tenant cases to be initiated (one Nonpayment case and two Holdover cases). He also brings in a check for $132.25 to cover all initiation fees for the three cases.

39. Based on the preceding procedure and situation, which of the following statements regarding the processing of the cases by Court Officer Wilma Chin is most correct?
A. Court Officer Wilma Chin should initiate the three cases and collect the fee of $132.25, which is the same amount as the check.
B. The $6.75 fee may be waived because the increase takes effect on July 22, 2019.
C. The correct total amount the Court Officer Chin should collect is $125.50.
D. Court Officer Chin should inform the attorney that the fees for the three cases is $6.75 more than the check amount.

39. Answer: D
Correct choice is D. Court Officer Chin should inform the attorney that the fees for the three cases is $6.75 more than the check amount.

Fees:
Nonpayment ($30.00 + 2.25 + 6.75 = $39.00)
Holdover: ($40.00 + $3.25 + 6.75 = $50.00 X 2 cases = $100.00)

$39.00 + $100.00 = Total of $139.00 fees for all three cases.

•

40. Situation:
Sam Tasmin, a landlord, wishes to initiate a Landlord and Tenant Nonpayment case. He hands Court Officer Chin the required papers and a check for $32.25. He states that he is not paying the postage fee because he wishes to deliver the papers to the tenant himself.

30. Based on the preceding procedure and situation, which of the following statements regarding the processing of the cases by Court Officer Wilma Chin is most correct?

A. Court Officer Chin should process the papers, collect the $32.25 fee, and permit Mr. Tasmin to deliver the papers himself.
B. Court Officer Chin should inform Mr. Tasmin that the correct fee is $50.00.
C. Court Officer Chin should inform Mr. Tasmin that the correct fee is $39.00 and that the court will deliver the papers by mail.
D. Court Officer Chin should inform Mr. Tasmin that he should hire a lawyer since he does not understand the case initiation procedures.

40. Answer: C. Court Officer Chin should inform Mr. Tasmin that the correct fee is $39.00.

Choice "A" is wrong because the procedure does not mention that the person can deliver the papers himself.

Choice "B" is wrong because the correct fee is: Nonpayment ($30.00 + 2.25 + 6.75 = $39.00)

Choice "D" is wrong because according to the procedure, there is no requirement that Mr. Tasmin hire a lawyer.

Remembering facts and information

NOTE: On the actual exam, this section, "Remembering facts and information," is usually given first.

How this portion of the test is usually administered:

"You will be provided with a written description of an incident (story) on a one page form and given five (5) minutes to read and study the story.
At the end of the 5-minute period, the story will be removed and you will not have another opportunity to refer back to it.
You will not be permitted to make any written notes about the story.
There will be a 10-minute delay before you receive your test question booklet.
You will then be asked a series of questions about the facts concerning the story."(1)

Other details:
The passage is usually under one page long (approximately 300-400 words).
A typical candidate can read the passage carefully 2-3 times within the allotted 5 minutes.
The number of questions that are asked is usually about 10 to 15.

Directions:

When instructed by the test monitor, turn this page over and for the next 5 minutes, read the passage on the page as many times as you want. Try to memorize as many details of the passage as you can. At the end of the 5 minutes, when the test monitor instructs you to do so, stop reading and turn the page over. The test monitor will then collect this page.

(After the next 10 minutes, the test monitor will distribute the test booklets. When instructed to do so by the test monitor, open the test booklet and answer the first 15 questions in the booklet.)

On January 21, 2019, seven inches of snow had already covered the sidewalks by 8:30 a.m. Court Officer Helen Jennings, who lived only six blocks from the criminal court building in downtown Brooklyn, received a phone call from her Lieutenant, James Cordan, who was confirming that she would be coming to work, since more than half of the Court Officers in the command had already called that they would be unable to make the commute to work. Officer Jennings told her Lieutenant that she was just about to leave her house and that she would arrive at the court house before 9 a.m. On the way to the courthouse, Court Officer Jennings purchased a coffee and a bagel at City Donut, one block away from the criminal court building. When she arrived at the building at 279 Worthman Street, she noticed that two of the four magnetometers situated at the entrance of the building were not in operation and that each of the other two active magnetometers had only one Court Officer attending to it. The two Court Officers gave her a warm greeting. Court Officer Lance Thomas told her that so far only twelve Court Officers (including Court Officer Jennings) had arrived and that only three of the twenty-two judges had made it in. Court Officer Theresa Ming said that Major Kensington called that he was about twenty blocks away and that he would be arriving at about 9:30 a.m.

Court Officer Jennings quickly got into her uniform and reported to Lieutenant Cordan at 8:58 a.m. For most of the morning, Court Officer Jennings by herself did security patrol on floors 2, 3, and 4, something that was usually done by three Court Officers. Fortunately, only three of the fifteen parts were open on those floors, and the number of people was only about twenty percent of normal volume. Court Officer Jennings worked through lunch and then worked in Trial Part 26 in the afternoon. The Judge in the Part 26, Judge Manuel Thompson, thanked her for coming to work, as did Major Kensington during his afternoon rounds of the building. Most of the Court Officers who had long commutes left at 5:00 p.m. However, because Court Officer Jennings lived nearby, she volunteered for the 5:00 p.m. - 6:00 p.m. security detail. Although the snow was still coming down when she left at 6:15 p.m., she arrived home at 6:40 p.m.

41. The address of the Criminal Court building is:
    A. 259 Workman Street
    B. 295 Workmen Street
    C. 297 Worthmen Street
    D. 279 Worthman Street

42. The last name of the Major referred to in the passage is:
    A. Cordan
    B. Ming
    C. Kensington
    D. Thompson

43. Court Officer Jennings bought a coffee and bagel at:
    A. NYC Donut Shop
    B. City Donut
    C. City Donuts and Bagels
    D. NYC Coffee Shop

44. How many magnetometers were located at the entrance of the criminal court building?
    A. three
    B. two
    C. four
    D. none of the above

45. Most of the Court Officers who had long commutes left at:
    A. 5:00 p.m.
    B. 5:30 p.m.
    C. 6:00 p.m.
    D. 6:15 p.m.

46. The passage describes incidents that happened on what date?
    A. January 21, 2018
    B. January 21, 2019
    C. January 12, 2018
    D. January 12, 2019

47. In what number part did Court Officer Jennings work in the afternoon?
    A. Part 9
    B. Part 29
    C. Part 26
    D. Part 6

48. The volume of people in the afternoon was _____ percent of the usual volume.
    A. ten percent
    B. twenty percent
    C. thirty percent
    D. forty percent

49. How many inches of snow had covered the sidewalk by 8:30 a.m.?
    A. three
    B. four
    C. six
    D. seven

50. Which Court Officer said that Major Kensington called that he was about twenty blocks away?
    A. Court Officer Cordan
    B. Court Officer Theresa Ming
    C. Court Officer Thomas
    D. Court Officer Madison

51. Court Officer Jennings arrived at home at:
    A. 5:40 p.m.
    B. 6:00 p.m.
    C. 6:40 p.m.
    D. 6:00 a.m.

52. The last name of the judge in Part 26 was:
    A. Thomas
    B. Thompson
    C. Kensington
    D. Cordan

53. What did Court Officer Jennings purchase on her way to work?
    A. Tea and donut
    B. Coffee and bagel
    C. Coffee and jelly donut
    D. Coffee and muffin

54. How far away from the coffee shop was the court building?
    A. three blocks
    B one block
    C. two blocks
    D. none of the above

55. What was the number of total Parts open on floors 2, 3 and 4?
    A. 3
    B. seven
    C. 15
    D. none of the above

Questions 56-70

Directions:
The following 15 questions are based on the following three tables (Daily Log of Cases - Civil Court; Daily Log of Cases - Criminal Court; Daily Log of Cases - Family Court). First, fill-in the two cells with the notations "1?" and "2?", then answer the 15 questions based on the information in the three tables. Two supplementary tables, "Daily Breakdown of Cases (Civil Court, Criminal Court and Family Court"; and "Summary of Cases (Civil Court, Criminal Court and Family Court)" are provided to help you organize the information so that you will be able to answer the questions correctly. Only the answers will be graded.

The following is a log of cases in Civil Court Conference Parts on September 12, 2019. Cases are conferenced in these Parts and they are either "Adjourned", "Dismissed" or "Settled" (settled with a money award, or settled-with no money award).

Daily Log of Cases - September 12, 2019 Civil Court			
Judge	**Date Filed**	**Status**	**Money Award**
Rampor ✔	06/12/17 ✔	Settled ✔	X
Thompson ✔	04/08/18 ✔	Dismissed ✔	X
Wang ✔	01/05/19 ✔	**Settled** (1?) ✔	$15,400
Thompson ✔	06/25/18 ✔	Settled ✔	X
Thompson ✔	09/22/18 ✔	Adjourned ✔	X
Rampor ✔	08/17/18 ✔	Dismissed ✔	X
Wang ✔	09/21/17 ✔	Adjourned ✔	X
Rampor ✔	11/15/18 ✔	Adjourned ✔	X
Thompson ✔	11/15/17 ✔	Settled ✔	$13,500
Rampor ✔	07/19/18 ✔	Adjourned ✔	X
Wang ✔	02/16/19 ✔	Dismissed ✔	X
Thompson ✔	09/27/17 ✔	Settled ✔	$17,200
Wang ✔	06/10/18 ✔	Settled ✔	$24,500
Rampor ✔	05/13/17 ✔	Adjourned ✔	X
Thompson ✔	02/09/18 ✔	Settled ✔	$22,900

The following is a log of cases of Criminal Court Cases on September 12, 2019. Cases appeared in front of the following judges and were "Adjourned", "Dismissed", or "Disposed" (with either a jail "Sentence" or with "No sentence").

Daily Log of Cases - September 12, 2019 Criminal Court			
Judge	**Date Filed**	**Status**	**Sentence**
Wilks ✔	05/13/18 ✔	**Disposed** (2?) ✔	Sentence
Rodriguez ✔	03/07/19 ✔	Adjourned ✔	X
Cohen ✔	02/04/19 ✔	Adjourned ✔	X
Rodriguez ✔	05/24/19 ✔	Disposed ✔	No Sentence
Rodriguez ✔	08/21/18 ✔	Adjourned ✔	X
Wilks ✔	07/18/19 ✔	Dismissed ✔	X
Cohen ✔	08/20/17 ✔	Adjourned ✔	X
Wilks ✔	04/14/19 ✔	Disposed ✔	Sentence
Rodriguez ✔	06/16/18 ✔	Dismissed ✔	X
Wilks ✔	05/18/18 ✔	Disposed ✔	Sentence
Cohen ✔	04/15/19 ✔	Adjourned ✔	X
Rodriguez ✔	07/26/19 ✔	Disposed ✔	No sentence
Cohen ✔	05/11/17 ✔	Disposed ✔	Sentence
Wilks ✔	04/12/18 ✔	Dismissed ✔	X
Cohen ✔	02/09/19 ✔	Adjourned ✔	X

On the following pages, there are tables for "Daily Log of Cases Logs of Family Court" for September 12, 2019 and blank "Summary of Cases September 12, 2019" (Civil, Criminal and Family Courts).

Cases in Family Court that were not "Adjourned" or "Dismissed" were "Disposed" (either through "Hearing Complete" or "PINS Referral").

Daily Log of Cases - September 12, 2019
Family Court

Judge	Date Filed	Status	Completion
Baker ✔	02/11/17 ✔	Dismissed ✔	X
Visilov ✔	02/05/19 ✔	Adjourned ✔	X
Ruggiero ✔	01/07/18 ✔	Disposed ✔	PINS Referral
Ruggiero ✔	03/21/19 ✔	Adjourned ✔	X
Baker ✔	06/19/18 ✔	Dismissed ✔	X
Visilov ✔	02/12/19 ✔	Disposed ✔	PINS Referral
Baker ✔	06/22/18 ✔	Disposed ✔	Hearing Complete
Ruggiero ✔	03/09/19 ✔	Dismissed ✔	X
Visilov ✔	04/15/18 ✔	Adjourned ✔	X
Ruggiero ✔	06/19/19 ✔	Disposed ✔	Hearing Complete
Visilov ✔	02/13/19 ✔	Adjourned ✔	X
Baker ✔	05/12/17 ✔	Disposed ✔	Hearing Complete
Baker ✔	07/16/19 ✔	Dismissed ✔	X
Visilov ✔	03/13/18 ✔	Disposed ✔	PINS Referral
Baker ✔	06/11/19 ✔	Disposed ✔	PINS Referral

Summary of Cases September 12, 2019
(Civil, Criminal and Family Courts)

Status of Case	Civil	Criminal	Family	Cases Total
Adjourned						5							6					4	15
Dismissed	||| 3	||| 3	|||| 4	10
Disposed - Sentence		|||| 4		4
Disposed - No Sentence		|| 2		2
Disposed - Hearing Complete			||| 3	3
Disposed - PINS Referral			|||| 4	4
Settled - No money Award	|| 2			2
Settled - Money Award	||||| 5			5
Total Cases	15	15	15	45
Cases Filed by Year				
2017						5			2			2	9
2018									8						5						5	18
2019			2									8									8	18
Total Cases	15	15	15	45

Judge	Dismissed	Adjourned	Settled With No Money Award	Settled With Money Award	Disposed With PINS Referral	Disposed Hearing Complete	Disposed With Sentence	Disposed With No Sentence	Total Cases
			Summary of Cases (Civil, Criminal, Family)						
Rampor	| 1	||| 3	| 1						5
Thompson	| 1	| 1	| 1	||| 3					6
Wang	| 1	| 1		|| 2					4
Wilks	|| 2						||| 3		5
Rodriguez	| 1	|| 2						|| 2	5
Cohen		||||| 4					| 1		5
Baker	||| 3				| 1	|| 2			6
Visilov		||| 3			|| 2				5
Ruggiero	| 1	| 1			| 1	| 1			4
									<u>45</u>

56. The total number of criminal court adjourned cases exceeded the total number of family court adjourned cases by:
   A. 1
   B. 2 (Criminal court adjourned cases = 6, Family court adjourned cases = 4)
   C. 3
   D. none of the above

57. The total number of 2019 cases for Civil, Criminal, and Family Court is:
   A. 9
   B. 16
   C. 17
   D. 18 (Civil 2, plus Criminal 8, plus Family 8 =18)

58. How many cases were "Settled - Money Award"?
   A. 3
   B. 4
   C. 5
   D. 6

59. How many cases did Judge Thompson "Settle With Money Award"?
   A. 1
   B. 2
   C. 3
   D. none of the above

60. The total number of cases handled by Judges Baker and Visilov is:
   A. 10
   B. 11 (Baker 6 + Visilov 5 = 11)
   C. 12
   D. none of the above

61. Which two Judges tied for handling the greatest number of cases?
    A. Judge Wang and Judge Raynor   C. Judge Rodriguez and Judge Baker
    B. Judge Rampor and Judge Rodriguez **D. Judge Thompson and Judge Baker** (6)

62. What is the total number of adjourned cases for all 3 courts combined?
    A. 14   C. 16
    B. 15   D. none of the above

63. Which two Judges tied for the least number of cases handled?
    A. Judge Wang and Judge Ruggiero (4)
    B. Judge Visilov and Judge Cohen
    C. Judge Rampor and Judge Rodriguez
    D. Judge Wilks and Judges Ruggiero

64. What is the total number of cases for Civil Court plus Criminal Court?
    A. 15
    B. 30 (Civil 15 + Criminal 15 = 30)
    C. 45
    D. 60

65. How many cases were "Disposed With PINS Referral"?
    A. 2   **C. 4**
    B. 3   D. none of the above

66. What is the total number of cases handled by all three courts?
    A. 15
    B. 40
    C. 65
    D. none of the above (Correct total is 45 cases.)

67. Which court dismissed the greatest number of cases?
    A. Family court (Dismissed 4 cases.)
    B. Criminal court
    C. Family court
    D. none of the above. All three courts dismissed an equal number of cases.

68. The total number of 2018 cases handled by all courts exceeded the total number of 2017 cases by:
    A. 9 (2017 = 9; 2018 cases = 18)
    B. 18
    C. 26
    D. 8

69. How many Family court cases were "Disposed - PINS Referral"?
    A. 2   **C. 4**
    B. 3   D. 5

70. What is the total of 2017 cases and 2018 cases?
    A. 36   C. 9
    B. 18   **D. 27** (9 + 18 = 27)

ANSWER KEY- PRACTICE TEST

1. A	26. D	51. C
2. B	27. C	52. B
3. D	28. B	53. B
4. C	29. D	54. B
5. B	30. B	55. A
6. D	31. D	56. B
7. D	32. B	57. D
8. C	33. D	58. C
9. A	34. B	59. C
10. B	35. D	60. B
11. B	36. C	61. D
12. B	37. C	62. B
13. C	38. D	63. A
14. D	39. D	64. B
15. A	40. C	65. C
16. C	41. D	66. D
17. A	42. C	67. A
18. B	43. B	68. A
19. D	44. C	69. C
20. C	45. A	70. D
21. D	46. B	
22. B	47. C	
23. A	48. B	
24. C	49. D	
25. C	50. B	

Made in the USA
Middletown, DE
04 December 2020